Better Homes and Gardens®

Hometown

FAVORITES

Delicious down-home recipes

Volume 8

Meredith Consumer Marketing
Des Moines, Iowa

Better Homes and Gardens®

Hometown Favorites

MEREDITH CONSUMER MARKETING
Consumer Marketing Product Director: Heather Sorensen
Consumer Marketing Product Manager: Wendy Merical
Consumer Marketing Billing/Renewal Manager: Tami Beachem
Business Director: Ron Clingman
Senior Production Manager: Al Rodruck

WATERBURY PUBLICATIONS, INC.
Editorial Director: Lisa Kingsley
Associate Editor: Tricia Bergman
Associate Editor/Food Stylist: Annie Peterson
Assistant Food Stylist: Skyler Myers
Creative Director: Ken Carlson
Associate Design Director: Doug Samuelson
Production Assistant: Mindy Samuelson
Indexer: Mary Williams
Contributing Food Stylist: Charlie Worthington
Contributing Copy Editors: Terri Fredrickson, Peg Smith

BETTER HOMES AND GARDENS® MAGAZINE
Editor in Chief: Stephen Orr
Deputy Editor, Food and Entertaining: Nancy Wall Hopkins

MEREDITH NATIONAL MEDIA GROUP
President: Tom Harty

MEREDITH CORPORATION
Chairman and Chief Executive Officer: Stephen M. Lacy

In Memoriam: E.T. Meredith III (1933–2003)

Test Kitchen

Our seal assures you that every recipe in *Hometown Favorites* has been tested in the Better Homes and Gardens® Test Kitchen. This means that each recipe is practical and reliable, and it meets our high standards of taste appeal. We guarantee your satisfaction with this book for as long as you own it.

All of us at Meredith Consumer Marketing are dedicated to providing you with information and ideas to enhance your home. We welcome your comments and suggestions. Write to us at: Meredith Consumer Marketing, 1716 Locust St., Des Moines, IA 50309-3023.

Pictured on front cover:
Sherried Cherry Crisp, page 174
Photography by Blaine Moats

Contents

CHAPTER 1

Appetizers

Host a casual gathering, throw a party, or head to a potluck with these enticing bites and drinks that make the event even more special.

Italian Beef Sliders with Pepperoncini Slaw

These flavor-packed sliders come together quickly with cooked roast beef. The crunchy slaw topping gets a pleasant touch of heat from pepperoncini peppers.

1. Place beef and juices in a medium saucepan; break up any large pieces. Add vegetables, half the Italian seasoning, and the crushed red pepper. Heat through.

2. Meanwhile, for slaw, in a medium bowl combine coleslaw mix, pepperoncini peppers and liquid, and the remaining Italian seasoning.

3. Spoon beef and vegetable filling on roll bottoms. Top with coleslaw; add roll tops.

PER SERVING *148 cal., 4 g fat (1 g sat. fat), 21 mg chol., 347 mg sodium, 18 g carb., 1 g fiber, 10 g pro.*

START TO FINISH **20 minutes**

12 servings	ingredients	24 servings
one 17-oz. pkg.	refrigerated cooked beef roast au jus	two 17-oz. pkg.
2 cups	frozen sweet pepper and onion strips	4 cups
1 tsp.	dried Italian seasoning, crushed	2 tsp.
⅛ to ¼ tsp.	crushed red pepper	¼ to ½ tsp.
2 cups	coleslaw mix (shredded cabbage with carrot)	4 cups
½ cup	pepperoncini salad peppers, stemmed and chopped, plus 2 Tbsp. drained liquid	1 cup
12	2- to 3-inch rolls, split	24

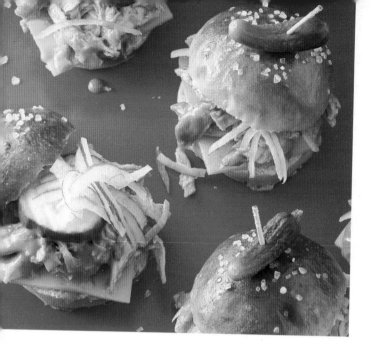

BBQ Chicken Sliders

No leftover cooked chicken on hand? Pick up a rotisserie chicken from a grocery store for the filling in these sliders.

1. In a medium saucepan combine chicken, barbecue sauce, mustard, brown sugar, and barbecue seasoning. Cook over medium heat until heated through, stirring frequently.

2. If desired, brush the cut sides of buns with melted butter. Toast buns, cut sides down, on a griddle or grill pan over medium heat until golden.

3. Place a slice of cheese on the bottom of each bun. Top with chicken and, if desired, onion and pickles. Replace tops of buns.

PER SERVING *257 cal., 9 g fat (4 g sat. fat), 55 mg chol., 909 mg sodium, 30 g carb., 1 g fiber, 14 g pro.*

START TO FINISH **30 minutes**

12 servings	ingredients	24 servings
2½ cups	shredded cooked chicken	5 cups
¾ cup	barbecue sauce	1½ cups
¼ cup	yellow mustard	½ cup
2 Tbsp.	packed brown sugar	¼ cup
1 tsp.	barbecue seasoning	2 tsp.
12	pretzel or regular cocktail buns, split	24
2 Tbsp.	butter, melted (optional)	¼ cup
12 small slices	sharp cheddar cheese	24 small slices
	Slivered red onion (optional)	
	Dill pickle or bread-and-butter pickle slices (optional)	

Buffalo Chicken Wings with Blue Cheese Dressing

This tried-and-true party food is guaranteed to be a hit. The best part? The wings and dip can be ready to serve in a mere 30 minutes.

1. In a large bowl combine half the cayenne pepper sauce, half the cider vinegar, the garlic powder, and the ginger. Add drummettes; toss to coat.

2. Arrange drummettes on the unheated rack of a broiler pan. Broil 4 to 5 inches from the heat for 15 to 20 minutes or until chicken is tender and no longer pink, turning once. Drizzle chicken with remaining cayenne pepper sauce and cider vinegar.

3. Meanwhile, in a bowl stir together sour cream, blue cheese, green onion, white wine vinegar, lemon juice, and sugar. Serve chicken drummettes with dressing and carrot and celery sticks.

PER SERVING *228 cal., 14 g fat (5 g sat. fat), 67 mg chol., 260 mg sodium, 7 g carb., 1 g fiber, 17 g pro.*

START TO FINISH **30 minutes**

8 servings	ingredients	16 servings
4 Tbsp.	bottled cayenne pepper sauce	½ cup
2 tsp.	cider vinegar	4 tsp.
½ tsp.	garlic powder	1 tsp.
½ tsp.	ground ginger	1 tsp.
24	chicken drummettes	48
¾ cup	fat-free sour cream	1½ cups
½ cup	crumbled blue cheese	1 cup
2 Tbsp.	sliced green onion	¼ cup
1 Tbsp.	white wine vinegar	2 Tbsp.
1 Tbsp.	lemon juice	2 Tbsp.
1 tsp.	sugar	2 tsp.
	Carrot and celery sticks	

Tequila Shrimp Nachos

This fresh spin on classic nachos is sure to excite party-goers. Make it in late summer and early fall, when the tastiest tomatoes are at their peak.

1. Thaw shrimp, if frozen. For marinade, with a mortar and pestle crush cumin seeds; transfer to a large bowl. Whisk in orange juice, half the tequila, and the ground ancho chile pepper. Add shrimp and toss to coat. Let stand for 15 minutes, stirring twice.

2. Meanwhile, cut heirloom tomatoes into wedges. On a large platter arrange tomato wedges and halved tomatoes; set aside. For vinaigrette, in a screw-top jar with lid combine 4 tablespoons of the oil, the remaining tequila, the lime juice, garlic, and salt. Cover and shake well to combine.

3. Drain shrimp, discarding marinade. Place shrimp in a large grill basket. Brush roma tomatoes and jalapeño halves with remaining oil. Grill shrimp in basket, and the tomatoes and jalapeños on grill rack, covered, over medium heat for 5 to 7 minutes or until shrimp are opaque and tomatoes and jalapeño halves are slightly soft and lightly browned, stirring shrimp occasionally. Place shrimp in a bowl. When cool enough to handle, finely chop jalapeño halves and stir into shrimp.

4. Add shrimp with jalapeños and grilled tomatoes to platter. Drizzle with vinaigrette. Top with cilantro and, if desired, queso fresco. Serve immediately or cover and chill up to 4 hours.

*TIP Chile peppers contain oils that can irritate skin and eyes. Wear plastic or rubber gloves when working with them.

FOR 20 SERVINGS In Step 2, use 8 tablespoons of the oil.

PER SERVING *160 cal., 8 g fat (1 g sat. fat), 114 mg chol., 580 mg sodium, 6 g carb., 1 g fiber, 13 g pro.*

PREP **35 minutes**
MARINATE **15 minutes**
GRILL **5 minutes**

10 servings	ingredients	20 servings
2 lb.	fresh or frozen medium shrimp, peeled and deveined	4 lb.
1 tsp.	cumin seeds	2 tsp.
½ cup	orange juice	1 cup
4 Tbsp.	tequila	½ cup
½ tsp.	ground ancho chile pepper or hot chili powder	1 tsp.
2 to 3	medium heirloom tomatoes	4 to 6
1½ cups	red and/or yellow pear-shape, grape, and/or cherry tomatoes, halved	3 cups
5 Tbsp.	olive oil	10 Tbsp.
2 Tbsp.	lime juice	¼ cup
1 large clove	garlic, minced	2 large cloves
¼ tsp.	salt	½ tsp.
5	roma tomatoes, halved	10
1	fresh jalapeño, halved and seeded*	2
2 Tbsp.	snipped fresh cilantro	¼ cup
1 oz.	queso fresco or feta, crumbled (optional)	2 oz.

Shrimp with Asian Cocktail Sauce

This version of the classic appetizer that originated in the early 20th century features a sprinkle of toasted sesame seeds for a nutty finish.

1. Thaw shrimp, if frozen. Peel and devein shrimp, leaving tails intact. Rinse shrimp; pat dry with paper towels. Sprinkle shrimp with salt.

2. Lightly coat a grill pan or large skillet with cooking spray; heat over medium-high heat. Add shrimp; cook 6 to 8 minutes or until shrimp are opaque, turning once. Sprinkle with toasted sesame seeds.

3. Meanwhile, for sauce, in a small bowl combine the remaining ingredients. Serve shrimp with sauce.

*TIP To toast whole nuts or large pieces, spread them in a shallow pan. Bake in a 350°F oven for 5 to 10 minutes, shaking the pan once or twice. Toast coconut in the same way, watching closely to prevent burning. Toast small amounts of finely chopped nuts, coconut, or seeds in a dry skillet over medium heat for 2 minutes or until fragrant and golden, stirring frequently.

PER SERVING *107 cal., 1 g fat (0 g sat. fat), 86 mg chol., 406 mg sodium, 10 g carb., 1 g fiber, 12 g pro.*

START TO FINISH **30 minutes**

6 servings	ingredients	12 servings
18	fresh or frozen jumbo shrimp in shells (about 1 pound)	36
⅛ tsp.	salt	¼ tsp.
	Nonstick cooking spray	
1 tsp.	sesame seeds, toasted*	2 tsp.
one 8-oz. can	no-salt-added tomato sauce	one 15-oz. can
2 Tbsp.	finely chopped red onion	¼ cup
2 Tbsp.	bottled plum sauce	¼ cup
2 Tbsp.	bottled chili sauce	¼ cup
1 Tbsp.	rice vinegar	2 Tbsp.
2 tsp.	reduced-sodium soy sauce	4 tsp.
½ tsp.	orange zest	1 tsp.

Bacon-Stuffed Mushrooms

Smoky bacon makes these cheese-stuffed mushrooms especially decadent and irresistible. With only five ingredients, this recipe is simple and quick.

1. Preheat oven to 350°F. Lightly grease a 15×10×1-inch baking pan. In a large skillet cook bacon until almost crisp. Using a slotted spoon, remove bacon from skillet; discard fat. Drain bacon on paper towels.

2. Clean mushrooms; remove and discard stems.

3. For filling, in a medium bowl stir together cream cheese and cheddar cheese. Stir in reserved bacon and, if desired, garlic. Spoon filling into mushroom tops, then place in prepared baking pan.

4. Bake 25 to 30 minutes or until mushrooms are tender. Let stand for 5 minutes before serving.

TO MAKE AHEAD Assemble mushrooms then refrigerate, covered, up to 24 hours.

FOR 20 SERVINGS Use two 15×10×1-inch baking pans or bake in two batches.

PER SERVING *75 cal., 6 g fat (3 g sat. fat), 18 mg chol., 155 mg sodium, 1 g carb., 0 g fiber, 4 g pro.*

PREP 25 minutes
BAKE 25 minutes
STAND 5 minutes

10 servings	ingredients	20 servings
6 slices	bacon, cut into ¼-inch pieces	12 slices
10 large	fresh mushrooms	20 large
3 oz.	cream cheese, softened	6 oz.
¼ cup	shredded sharp cheddar or smoked Gouda cheese	½ cup
½ tsp.	minced garlic (optional)	1 tsp.

Potato Pancakes with Herbed Crème

PREP 30 minutes
BAKE 14 minutes

22 servings	ingredients	44 servings
	Nonstick olive oil cooking spray	
1	egg, lightly beaten	2
2 Tbsp.	all-purpose flour	¼ cup
1 tsp.	salt	2 tsp.
½ tsp.	black pepper	1 tsp.
1 lb.	russet potatoes	2 lbs.
1½ cups	finely shredded zucchini	3 cups
1 cup	finely shredded carrots	2 cups
½ cup	plain low-fat yogurt	1 cup
2 Tbsp.	finely snipped fresh basil	¼ cup
1 Tbsp.	finely snipped fresh chives	2 Tbsp.

These potato pancakes, with the addition of carrots and zucchini, are topped with a tangy yogurt sauce. Speed prep by using a food processor to shred the vegetables.

1. Preheat oven to 425°F. Line an extra-large baking sheet with parchment paper; coat with cooking spray. In a bowl whisk together egg, flour, salt, and pepper.

2. Peel and finely shred potatoes. Press shredded potatoes between several layers of paper towels to remove excess moisture. In a bowl combine shredded potatoes, zucchini, and carrots. Add egg mixture; stir just until combined.

3. Drop potato mixture by rounded tablespoons onto the prepared baking sheet. Using the back of a spoon, slightly flatten mounds. Coat mounds with cooking spray. Bake 7 minutes. Turn pancakes; bake 7 minutes more or until lightly browned.

4. Meanwhile, for Herbed Crème, combine yogurt, basil, and chives. Serve with warm potato pancakes.

PER SERVING *25 cal., 0 g fat, 10 mg chol., 118 mg sodium, 4 g carb., 1 g fiber, 1 g pro.*

Cheeseburger and Fries Dip

For a fun presentation, serve this dip with a variety of French-fried potatoes from a supermarket's freezer section.

1. In a large skillet cook beef, onion, and garlic over medium-high heat until meat is browned. Drain off fat.

2. In a 1½- or 2-quart slow cooker combine meat mixture, pasteurized cheese, tomato, tomato paste, mustard, and Worcestershire sauce. Cover and cook on low for 3 to 4 hours or on high for 1½ to 2 hours. If needed, stir in milk to reach desired consistency.

3. Serve immediately or keep warm, covered, on warm setting (if available) up to 2 hours, stirring occasionally. If desired, top with pickle slices. Serve with baked waffle- or french fry-cut potatoes.

FOR 32 SERVINGS In Step 2, use a 3½- or 4-quart slow cooker.

PER SERVING *125 cal., 8 g fat (4 g sat. fat), 35 mg chol., 401 mg sodium, 4 g carb., 1 g fiber, 10 g pro.*

PREP 20 minutes
SLOW COOK 3 hours (low) or 1½ hours (high)

16 servings	ingredients	32 servings
1 lb.	lean ground beef	2 lbs.
1 cup	chopped onion	2 cups
1 clove	garlic, minced	2 cloves
12 oz.	pasteurized prepared cheese product (Velveeta), cut up	24 oz.
⅔ cup	chopped tomato	1⅓ cups
half 6-oz. can	tomato paste	one 6-oz. can
3 Tbsp.	yellow mustard	6 Tbsp.
2 tsp.	Worcestershire sauce	4 tsp.
2 to 3 Tbsp.	milk (optional)	4 to 6 Tbsp.
	Pickle slices (optional)	
	Waffle- or french fry-cut potatoes	

Baked Mozzarella and Tomato-Basil Antipasti

Look for tiny balls of fresh mozzarella—boccocini—with the artisan cheeses at larger supermarkets or at specialty food stores.

1. Preheat oven to 350°F. In four 12- to 16-oz. ovenproof dishes or one 1½-quart shallow ovenproof dish layer pasta sauce, garlic, and mozzarella. Bake 20 minutes or until mozzarella is melted. Remove from oven; drizzle with the 1 tablespoon olive oil. Top with basil.

2. Lightly brush baguette slices with additional olive oil; place in a single layer on a large baking sheet. Broil 3 to 4 inches from heat for 2 minutes. Turn slices; sprinkle lightly with shredded Parmesan and dried basil. Broil 1 to 2 minutes more or until lightly toasted. Serve with baked mozzarella.

TO MAKE AHEAD Baguette slices can be broiled, cooled, and stored in an airtight container at room temperature up to 3 days.

FOR 8 SERVINGS In Step 1 use 2 tablespoons olive oil.

PER SERVING *201 cal., 10 g fat (4 g sat. fat), 23 mg chol., 527 mg sodium, 17 g carb., 1 g fiber, 8 g pro.*

PREP **15 minutes**
BAKE **20 minutes** BROIL **3 minutes**

4 servings	ingredients	8 servings
2 cups	pasta sauce	4 cups
1 clove	garlic, minced	2 cloves
8 oz.	bite-size fresh mozzarella balls, or mozzarella cheese, cubed	16 oz.
1 Tbsp.	olive oil	2 Tbsp.
¼ cup	torn fresh basil leaves	½ cup
1	baguette-style French bread, cut diagonally into ½-inch slices	2
	Olive oil	
	Finely shredded Parmesan cheese	
	Dried basil, crushed	

Hot Spinach-Artichoke Party Dip

This popular dip is extra delicious with three cheeses plus sour cream. Be sure the frozen spinach is completely thawed and all the excess moisture is squeezed out to prevent the dip from being watery.

1. Preheat oven to 350°F. In a large bowl beat cream cheese, sour cream, havarti, mustard, and grated Parmesan cheese with a mixer until combined.

2. Fold in spinach and artichoke hearts. Transfer to a deep 8-inch cast-iron skillet or 1½-quart casserole dish. Bake, uncovered, for 40 to 45 minutes or until heated through. Sprinkle with Parmesan shards and serve with tortilla chips and/or flatbread.

FOR 40 SERVINGS Use a deep 10-inch cast-iron skillet or 3-quart casserole dish.

PER SERVING *120 cal., 10 g fat (6 g sat. fat), 30 mg chol., 221 mg sodium, 2 g carb., 1 g fiber, 4 g pro.*

PREP 25 minutes
BAKE 40 minutes

20 servings	ingredients	40 servings
one 8-oz. pkg.	cream cheese, softened	two 8-oz. pkg.
1½ cups	sour cream	3 cups
6 oz.	Havarti cheese, shredded	12 oz.
1 Tbsp.	Dijon mustard	2 Tbsp.
½ cup	grated Parmesan cheese	1 cup
one 10-oz. pkg.	frozen chopped spinach, thawed and squeezed dry	two 10-oz. pkg.
one 14-oz. can	artichoke hearts, drained and chopped	two 14-oz. cans
	Parmesan cheese shards	
	Tortilla chips and/or flatbread	

Creamy Collard Dip

Inspired by Southern-style cuisine, this baked dip gets a kick from spicy Cajun seasoning. Pick the best collard greens you can find—they should be crisp and bright green with no signs of wilting or yellowing.

1. Preheat oven to 350°F. In an extra-large skillet cook bacon until crisp; drain on paper towels. Remove and discard all but 2 teaspoons bacon drippings from skillet. Add onion and sweet pepper to skillet. Cook 5 minutes over medium heat or just until vegetables are tender, stirring occasionally. Add collard greens and garlic; cover and cook 10 minutes or until tender, stirring occasionally. Remove from heat.

2. Add cream cheese, Monterey Jack cheese, sour cream, and Cajun seasoning to dip; stir until combined. If desired, trim and discard fatty part from bacon. Crumble remaining bacon and add to dip. Spread dip in a 1½-quart casserole dish.

3. Bake, uncovered, for 10 minutes or until warmed through. Serve with sweet pepper strips.

FOR 24 SERVINGS In Step 1 reserve 4 teaspoons bacon drippings. In Step 2 use a 3-quart casserole dish.

PER SERVING 104 cal., 8 g fat (4 g sat. fat), 23 mg chol., 208 mg sodium, 5 g carb., 1 g fiber, 5 g pro.

PREP 25 minutes
COOK 15 minutes
BAKE 10 minutes

12 servings	ingredients	24 servings
2 slices	bacon	4 slices
1 cup	chopped sweet onion	2 cups
¾ cup	seeded and chopped red sweet pepper	1½ cups
6 cups	trimmed and coarsely chopped fresh collard greens	12 cups
3 cloves	garlic, minced	6 cloves
one 8-oz. pkg.	reduced-fat cream cheese (Neufchâtel), cubed and softened	two 8-oz. pkg.
½ cup	shredded reduced-fat Monterey Jack cheese	1 cup
½ cup	light sour cream	1 cup
½ tsp.	Cajun seasoning	1 tsp.
	Sweet pepper strips	

Mediterranean Eggplant Dip

Grill the eggplant for a delicious hint of smokiness. For the best flavor, look for the freshest eggplant—it should be firm, free from brown spots, and heavy for its size.

1. In food processor finely chop garbanzo beans, mint leaves, and garlic. Add lemon juice, salt, and eggplant. With processor running, add the ¼ cup olive oil in a steady stream; process until smooth.

2. Transfer dip to a serving dish. Drizzle with additional olive oil. Garnish with snipped fresh mint and toasted walnuts. Serve with pita wedges.

* To grill eggplant, brush eight ½-inch eggplant slices with 2 tablespoons olive oil. Sprinkle with ½ teaspoon kosher salt. Grill, uncovered, over direct medium heat for 8 to 10 minutes or until tender, turning once. Cool slightly.

TO MAKE AHEAD Prepare dip as directed through Step 1. Place in airtight container; cover. Refrigerate up to 3 days. Transfer to serving dish. Before serving, let stand at room temperature for 30 minutes. Top as directed in Step 2.

FOR 28 SERVINGS In Step 1 use the ½ cup olive oil.

PER SERVING *79 cal., 6 g fat (1 g sat. fat), 0 mg chol., 190 mg sodium, 6 g carb., 2 g fiber, 1 g pro.*

PREP 20 minutes
GRILL 8 minutes

14 servings	ingredients	28 servings
1 cup	canned garbanzo beans (chickpeas), rinsed and drained	2 cups
1 Tbsp.	fresh mint leaves	2 Tbsp.
1 clove	garlic	2 cloves
1 Tbsp.	lemon juice	2 Tbsp.
½ tsp.	kosher salt	1 tsp.
1 cup	grilled eggplant cubes*	2 cups
¼ cup	olive oil	½ cup
	Olive oil	
	Snipped fresh mint	
	Chopped walnuts, toasted (tip, page 12)	
	Toasted pita wedges	

Roasted Red Pepper-Chipotle Hummus

Give traditional hummus a flavor upgrade by adding roasted sweet peppers and spicy chipotle peppers. Make extra and freeze some for last-minute appetizers.

1. In a food processor or blender combine garbanzo beans, red sweet pepper, tahini, lemon juice, garlic, chipotle pepper in adobo sauce, cumin, salt, and black pepper. Cover and process or blend until smooth, adding 1 tablespoon water at a time if necessary to reach desired consistency.

2. Spoon hummus into a serving bowl. If desired, drizzle with olive oil, sprinkle paprika, and/or chopped fresh cilantro or parsley. Serve with assorted dippers.

TO MAKE AHEAD Cover and chill hummus up to 3 days. Bring to room temperature to serve. Or place hummus in freezer container; freeze up to 1 month. Thaw overnight in refrigerator. Bring to room temperature to serve.

PER SERVING *184 cal., 7 g fat (1 g sat. fat), 0 mg chol., 235 mg sodium, 27 g carb., 4 g fiber, 6 g pro.*

START TO FINISH 20 minutes

8 servings	ingredients	16 servings
one 15-oz. can	garbanzo beans (chickpeas), rinsed and drained	two 15-oz. cans
½ cup	coarsely chopped bottled roasted red sweet pepper	1 cup
⅓ cup	tahini	⅔ cup
3 Tbsp.	lemon juice	6 Tbsp.
4 cloves	garlic	8 cloves
½ to 1	chipotle pepper in adobo sauce	1 to 2
1 tsp.	ground cumin	2 tsp.
¼ tsp.	salt	½ tsp.
⅛ tsp.	black pepper	¼ tsp.
	Olive oil, paprika, and/or chopped fresh cilantro or parsley (optional)	
	Dippers: Pita bread wedges or crisps, bagel chips, and/or cut-up vegetables (optional)	

Spicy Edamame Dip

Protein- and fiber-packed edamame beans—green soy beans picked before they completely mature—create a fresh bright green twist on bean dip.

1. In a saucepan cook edamame in a large amount of boiling water for 7 minutes. Drain, reserving 1 cup cooking liquid.

2. In a food processor combine cooked edamame, cilantro leaves, red onion, lime juice, Asian chili sauce, garlic, and kosher salt. Cover and process, slowly pouring in enough reserved cooking liquid to make a smooth dip; scrape down sides as needed. Cover and chill at least 1 hour before serving. Serve with cut-up vegetables.

FOR 20 SERVINGS In Step 1 reserve 2 cups cooking liquid.

PER SERVING *73 cal., 3 g fat (0 g sat. fat), 0 mg chol., 83 mg sodium, 8 g carb., 4 g fiber, 6 g pro.*

PREP **15 minutes**
COOK **7 minutes**
CHILL **1 hour**

10 servings	ingredients	20 servings
1 lb.	fresh or frozen shelled edamame	2 lb.
¼ cup	packed fresh cilantro leaves	½ cup
2 Tbsp.	chopped red onion	¼ cup
2 Tbsp.	lime juice	¼ cup
2 tsp.	Asian chili sauce (sriracha sauce)	4 tsp.
1 clove	garlic, sliced	2 cloves
¼ tsp.	kosher salt	½ tsp.
	Cut-up vegetables	

Cheesy Tomato Snack Mix

This bold Italian-style party mix features a crunchy blend of cereal, soy nuts, and cheese crackers seasoned with bits of dried tomato and Parmesan cheese.

1. Preheat oven to 300°F. In a large roasting pan combine the cereals, soy nuts, pretzels, and crackers.

2. In a small bowl combine oil, Italian seasoning, Parmesan cheese, dried tomatoes, Worcestershire sauce, and pepper. Pour over cereal mixture in pan; toss until well coated.

3. Bake, uncovered, for 30 minutes, stirring twice during baking. Spread snack mix on a large sheet of foil to cool.

PER SERVING *102 cal., 4 g fat (1 g sat. fat), 1 mg chol., 205 mg sodium, 15 g carb., 2 g fiber, 3 g pro.*

PREP 15 minutes
BAKE 30 minutes
COOL 30 minutes

24 servings	ingredients	48 servings
3 cups	bite-size square corn cereal	6 cups
3 cups	bite-size square rice cereal	6 cups
3 cups	bite-size square wheat cereal	6 cups
1 cup	salted roasted soy nuts or corn nuts	2 cups
1 cup	small fat-free pretzel knots	2 cups
1 cup	fish-shape cheddar cheese crackers	2 cups
¼ cup	olive oil or canola oil	½ cup
2 Tbsp.	dried Italian seasoning, crushed	¼ cup
2 Tbsp.	grated Parmesan cheese	¼ cup
2 Tbsp.	finely snipped dried tomatoes (not oil-packed)	¼ cup
1 Tbsp.	reduced-sodium Worcestershire sauce	2 Tbsp.
¼ tsp.	black pepper	½ tsp.

Herbed Mixed Nuts

These special roasted nuts get a boost—Italian-style—with the addition of grated Parmesan cheese and zesty herbs.

1. Preheat oven to 325°F. In a bowl combine melted butter, Worcestershire sauce, basil, and garlic salt. Add nuts; stir to coat.

2. Line a 15×10×1-inch baking pan with foil; spread nuts in pan. Sprinkle with Parmesan; stir gently to coat. Bake 15 minutes, stirring twice. Cool completely.

FOR 24 SERVINGS Use two 15×10×1-inch baking pans or bake nuts in two batches.

PER SERVING *189 cal., 15 g fat (2 g sat. fat), 3 mg chol., 76 mg sodium, 7 g carb., 4 g fiber, 8 g pro.*

PREP 10 minutes
BAKE 15 minutes

12 servings	ingredients	24 servings
1 Tbsp.	butter, melted	2 Tbsp.
1 Tbsp.	Worcestershire sauce	2 Tbsp.
2 tsp.	dried basil and/or oregano, crushed	4 tsp.
½ tsp.	garlic salt	1 tsp.
1 cup	whole walnuts	2 cups
1 cup	soy nuts	2 cups
1 cup	whole almonds	2 cups
2 Tbsp.	grated Parmesan cheese	¼ cup

Parmesan Shortbread Rounds

Keep these savory cookies on hand in the freezer for a ready-to-serve appetizer. Sweet apricot preserves counterbalance the rich cheesy flavor.

1. In a large bowl beat butter with a mixer on medium for 1 minute. Using a wooden spoon, stir in cheese. Stir in flour, paprika, and cayenne pepper until combined. Stir in pecans and chives to form a crumbly dough.

2. Turn dough out onto a lightly floured surface. Gently knead dough for 1 minute. Shape into a 12-inch log. Wrap log in plastic wrap; chill 8 hours or overnight.

3. Preheat oven to 325°F. Using a serrated knife, cut log into ¼-inch slices. Place slices 1 inch apart on an ungreased parchment-lined cookie sheet. Bake 15 to 17 minutes or until set. Remove rounds; cool on a wire rack.

4. If desired, serve with apricot preserves.

TO MAKE-AHEAD Layer rounds between sheets of waxed paper in an airtight container; cover. Refrigerate up to 3 days or freeze up to 3 months.

PER SERVING *103 cal., 7 g fat (3 g sat. fat), 13 mg chol., 103 mg sodium, 8 g carb., 1 g fiber, 3 g pro.*

PREP **25 minutes**
CHILL **8 hours**
BAKE **15 minutes per batch**

36 servings	ingredients	72 servings
¾ cup	butter, softened	1½ cups
2 cups	finely shredded Parmesan cheese (8 oz.)	4 cups
1¼ cups	all-purpose flour	2½ cups
1 Tbsp.	paprika	2 Tbsp.
¼ tsp.	cayenne pepper	½ tsp.
1 cup	finely chopped pecans	2 cups
2 Tbsp.	snipped fresh chives	¼ cup
	Apricot preserves (optional)	

Pineapple-Ginger Punch

Try this tropical spin on sangria at your next summer get-together. For extra convenience, make the ginger syrup to 3 days before serving the cocktails.

1. For ginger syrup, in a saucepan combine the water, sugar, and ginger. Bring to boiling, stirring until sugar is dissolved; reduce heat. Simmer, uncovered, 10 minutes. Cool ginger syrup to room temperature. Strain through a fine-mesh sieve into a bowl. If desired, add rum. Cover with plastic wrap; chill at least 2 hours.

2. In a large punch bowl or pitcher combine chilled ginger syrup, pineapple juice, lemon juice, and lime juice. Stir in club soda. Add ice cubes and lime slices and/or pineapple wedges.

TO MAKE AHEAD Prepare ginger syrup as directed in Step 1. Transfer to a glass jar; cover. Refrigerate up to 3 days.

PER SERVING *102 cal., 0 g fat, 0 mg chol., 30 mg sodium, 26 g carb., 1 g fiber, 1 g pro.*

PREP 20 minutes
COOL 1 hour
CHILL 2 hours

8 servings	ingredients	16 servings
1 cup	water	2 cups
½ cup	sugar	1 cup
⅔ cup	thinly sliced unpeeled fresh ginger	1⅓ cups
½ to 1 cup	rum or vodka (optional)	1 to 2 cups
2½ cups	unsweetened pineapple juice, chilled	5 cups
3 Tbsp.	lemon juice	6 Tbsp.
3 Tbsp.	lime juice	6 Tbsp.
one 1-liter bottle	club soda, chilled	two 1-liter bottles
	Ice cubes	
	Lime slices and/or pineapple wedges	

Orange-Strawberry Earl Grey Slush

Earl Grey tea is infused with bergamot, the peel from a small sour orange that gives the tea its signature flavor. In this fruity drink, it blends perfectly with sherbet and strawberries.

1. In a small saucepan bring the water to boiling. Remove from heat; add tea leaves. Cover and let stand 10 minutes. Pour tea through a fine-mesh strainer; discard tea leaves. Cool.

2. Pour 1 cup tea into ice cube trays. Freeze 3 hours or until firm. Chill remaining tea.

3. In a blender combine chilled tea, frozen strawberries, and orange sherbet. Cover; blend until smooth. With blender running add frozen tea cubes, a few at a time, until mixture is slushy.

4. Serve slush in tall chilled glasses. If desired, serve with strawberries and/or orange peel twists.

PER SERVING *123 cal., 1 g fat (1 g sat. fat), 0 mg chol., 34 mg sodium, 28 g carb., 3 g fiber, 1 g pro.*

PREP **20 minutes**
STAND **10 minutes**
FREEZE **3 hours**

3 servings	ingredients	6 servings
2½ cups	water	5 cups
4 tsp.	loose-leaf Earl Grey or English breakfast tea	8 tsp.
one 10- to 12-oz. pkg.	frozen unsweetened whole strawberries	two 10- to 12-oz. pkg.
1 cup	orange sherbet	2 cups
	Fresh strawberries and/or orange peel twists (optional)	

CHAPTER 2

Poultry

From family-friendly weeknight fare to company-special dinners, this lineup of chicken and turkey recipes offers plenty of delicious options.

32

38

63

Asian Drumsticks

The sweetness of pineapple-orange juice and brown sugar tames the heat of ginger and cayenne pepper in sauce for easy-to-make, oven-baked chicken.

PREP **15 minutes**
MARINATE **4 hours**
BAKE **40 minutes**

4 servings	ingredients	8 servings
8 to 12 (2 to 3 lb. total)	chicken drumsticks	16 to 24 (4 to 6 lb. total)
⅔ cup	frozen pineapple-orange juice concentrate, thawed	1⅓ cups
2 Tbsp.	soy sauce	¼ cup
1½ tsp.	ground ginger	3 tsp.
1 tsp.	garlic salt	2 tsp.
½ tsp.	cayenne pepper	1 tsp.
3 Tbsp.	packed brown sugar	6 Tbsp.
	Sliced green onions (optional)	
	Toasted sesame seeds (tip, page 12) (optional)	

1. Place chicken in a resealable plastic bag set in a shallow dish. For marinade, in a small bowl stir together juice concentrate, soy sauce, ginger, garlic salt, and cayenne pepper. Reserve ⅓ cup marinade for sauce. Pour remaining marinade over chicken. Seal bag; turn to coat chicken. Marinate in the refrigerator for 4 to 24 hours, turning bag occasionally.

2. For sauce, in a small bowl stir together reserved marinade and brown sugar; cover and chill until needed.

3. Preheat oven to 375°F. Drain chicken, discard marinade. Arrange chicken in a shallow baking pan. Bake 25 minutes. Brush both sides of chicken with some of the sauce. Bake 15 to 20 minutes more or until chicken is done (175°F), brushing once or twice with remaining sauce. If desired, sprinkle with green onions and sesame seeds.

FOR 8 SERVINGS In Step 1 reserve ⅔ cup marinade for the sauce.

PER SERVING *372 cal., 13 g fat (4 g sat. fat), 123 mg chol., 890 mg sodium, 31 g carb., 0 g fiber, 31 g pro.*

Chicken in Spiced Ancho-Peanut Sauce

The poblano is a mild chile pepper. Dried, it is called ancho chile pepper and is used to enhance foods with a fruity, slightly smoky flavor.

1. In a small bowl combine ancho pepper and enough hot water to cover. Let stand 15 minutes; drain and pat dry with paper towels. Cut pepper into small pieces.

2. Meanwhile, sprinkle chicken lightly with salt and black pepper. In a large skillet cook chicken in hot oil over medium to medium-high heat for 6 to 8 minutes or until golden brown, turning once. Remove chicken, reserving 2 tablespoons oil in skillet.

3. Add onion, garlic, and ancho pepper pieces to skillet. Cook over medium heat about 5 minutes or until onion is tender, stirring occasionally.

4. Transfer onion mixture to a food processor. Cover and pulse until a smooth paste forms. Add tomatoes, broth, the ½ cup peanuts, and the cinnamon. Cover and pulse until smooth. Return mixture to skillet; add chicken.

5. Bring to boiling; reduce heat. Simmer, uncovered, for 30 minutes or until chicken is done (175°F), turning once. Sprinkle with cilantro and, if desired, additional peanuts. If desired, serve with hot cooked rice.

FOR 12 SERVINGS In Step 2 reserve 4 tablespoons oil in skillet. In Step 4 use 1 cup peanuts.

PER SERVING *389 cal., 30 g fat (6 g sat. fat), 80 mg chol., 449 mg sodium, 11 g carb., 3 g fiber, 21 g pro.*

PREP 30 minutes
COOK 30 minutes

6 servings	ingredients	12 servings
1 large	dried ancho chile pepper, stemmed and seeded (tip, page 11)	2 large
6	bone-in chicken thighs, skinned if desired	12
	Salt	
	Black pepper	
¼ cup	vegetable oil	½ cup
½ cup	chopped onion	1 cup
3 cloves	garlic, minced	6 cloves
one 14.5-oz. can	fire-roasted diced tomatoes, drained	two 14.5-oz. cans
1 cup	chicken broth	2 cups
½ cup	dry roasted peanuts	1 cup
1 tsp.	ground cinnamon	2 tsp.
¼ cup	fresh cilantro sprigs	½ cup
	Chopped dry roasted peanuts (optional)	
	Hot cooked rice (optional)	

Chicken Cacciatore

This enduring favorite Italian-American dish features chicken gently braised in a savory mix of mushrooms, peppers, and tomatoes.

1. Sprinkle chicken lightly with salt and black pepper to taste. In a large skillet heat oil over medium heat. Add chicken; cook just until browned, turning once. Remove chicken from skillet.

2. In the same skillet combine mushrooms, sweet pepper, carrot, and garlic. Cook over medium heat for 4 minutes, stirring occasionally. Carefully add wine. Simmer, uncovered, until wine is nearly evaporated. Stir in tomatoes, onions, oregano, and coarse black pepper. Return chicken to skillet.

3. Simmer, covered, for 20 minutes or until chicken is done (175°F). Stir in vinegar. Season to taste with additional salt. If desired, sprinkle with olives and parsley before serving.

PER SERVING *317 cal., 9 g fat (2 g sat. fat), 129 mg chol., 609 mg sodium, 23 g carb., 4 g fiber, 31 g pro.*

PREP 20 minutes
COOK 30 minutes

4 servings	ingredients	8 servings
8 small (about 3 lb. total)	bone-in chicken thighs, skin removed	16 small (about 6 lb. total)
	Salt and black pepper	
1 Tbsp.	olive oil	2 Tbsp.
3 cups	sliced fresh cremini mushrooms	6 cups
1 large	green sweet pepper, seeded and cut into bite-size strips	2 large
⅓ cup	finely chopped carrot	⅔ cup
3 cloves	garlic, minced	6 cloves
½ cup	dry white wine or chicken broth	1 cup
one 28-oz. can	diced tomatoes, undrained	two 28-oz. cans
1½ cups	frozen small whole onions	3 cups
1 tsp.	dried oregano, crushed	2 tsp.
1 tsp.	coarse ground black pepper	2 tsp.
2 Tbsp.	balsamic vinegar	¼ cup
10	pitted kalamata olives, halved (optional)	20
⅓ cup	snipped fresh Italian parsley (optional)	⅔ cup

Brown Ale Braised Chicken

Brown ale delivers nutty caramel-like flavor to this braised chicken dish. Set aside the celery leaves to chop and sprinkle for a fresh finish.

1. Preheat oven to 350°F. In a small bowl combine brown sugar, chili powder, salt, crushed red pepper, and black pepper. Sprinkle on chicken; rub in with your fingers. Let stand for 10 minutes.

2. In an extra-large oven-going skillet heat oil over medium-high heat. Add chicken; cook until chicken is browned and skin is crisp, turning once. Remove chicken, reserving 1 tablespoon drippings in skillet.

3. Add carrots, chopped celery, and onion to the reserved drippings. Cook 5 minutes or just until vegetables are tender, stirring occasionally. Stir in flour; cook and stir for 1 minute. Stir in ale, broth, and garlic. Bring to simmering. Return chicken to skillet.

4. Cover skillet and transfer to oven. Bake 40 minutes or until chicken is done (175°F). Sprinkle with celery leaves and thyme.

FOR 8 SERVINGS In Step 2 reserve 2 tablespoons drippings in skillet.

PER SERVING *553 cal., 34 g fat (8 g sat. fat), 183 mg chol., 571 mg sodium, 23 g carb., 4 g fiber, 33 g pro.*

PREP **30 minutes**
STAND **10 minutes**
BAKE **40 minutes**

4 servings	ingredients	8 servings
1 Tbsp.	packed brown sugar	2 Tbsp.
1½ tsp.	chili powder	3 tsp.
½ tsp.	salt	1 tsp.
¼ tsp.	crushed red pepper	½ tsp.
¼ tsp.	black pepper	½ tsp.
8	bone-in chicken thighs	16
1 Tbsp.	vegetable oil	2 Tbsp.
8	small whole carrots with 1-inch tops	16
1 cup	chopped celery	2 cups
1	medium onion, sliced	2
2 Tbsp.	all-purpose flour	¼ cup
one 12-oz. bottle	brown ale	two 12-oz. bottles
½ cup	reduced-sodium chicken broth	1 cup
4 cloves	garlic, peeled	8 cloves
	Coarsely chopped celery leaves	
	Fresh thyme	

Basque Chicken

This traditional Mediterranean-style chicken stew is a hearty and delicious cool-weather dish.

1. Sprinkle chicken with half the salt and the black pepper. In a large Dutch oven heat oil over medium-high heat. Add chicken; cook 4 minutes or until lightly browned, turning once to brown evenly.

2. Add onion and sweet pepper to Dutch oven; cook 3 minutes or until crisp-tender. Add garlic; cook 30 seconds. Add tomatoes, potatoes, broth, fresh thyme, savory, and remaining salt. Bring to boiling; reduce heat. Simmer, covered, for 20 minutes or until chicken is no longer pink (175°F) and potatoes are tender. Remove from heat. Stir in olives. If desired, sprinkle with additional fresh thyme.

*TIP If desired, for 6 servings, substitute ¼ teaspoon dried thyme, crushed, for the fresh thyme. For 12 servings, substitute ½ teaspoon dried thyme, crushed, for the fresh thyme.

PER SERVING *204 cal., 6 g fat (1 g sat. fat), 79 mg chol., 576 mg sodium, 16 g carb., 3 g fiber, 21 g pro.*

START TO FINISH **30 minutes**

6 servings	ingredients	12 servings
1¼ lb.	skinless, boneless chicken thighs, cut into 2-inch pieces	2½ lb.
¼ tsp.	salt	½ tsp.
¼ tsp.	black pepper	½ tsp.
1 Tbsp.	olive oil	2 Tbsp.
1	onion, thinly sliced	2
1	red sweet pepper, cut into ¼-inch strips	2
2 cloves	garlic, minced	4 cloves
one 14.5-oz. can	diced tomatoes, drained	two 14.5-oz. cans
12 oz.	red potatoes, cut into ½-inch wedges and halved crosswise	24 oz.
1 cup	chicken broth	2 cups
1 tsp.	fresh snipped thyme*	2 tsp.
½ tsp.	dried savory, crushed	1 tsp.
¼ tsp.	salt	½ tsp.
⅓ cup	small pimiento-stuffed olives	⅔ cup
	Fresh thyme (optional)	

Roast Tarragon Chicken

The licorice-like flavor of tarragon lends subtle sweetness to this roasted chicken. Serve it with crusty bread, pasta, or rice to soak up the flavorful juices.

1. Preheat oven to 375°F. In a medium bowl combine oil, tarragon, garlic, salt, and pepper. Add tomatoes; toss gently to coat. Using a slotted spoon, transfer tomatoes to another bowl, reserving oil mixture. Add onions to oil mixture; toss gently to coat. Using the slotted spoon, transfer onions to another bowl, reserving oil mixture.

2. Arrange chicken in a shallow roasting pan. Brush chicken with the reserved oil mixture. Add onions to roasting pan.

3. Roast chicken and onions for 35 minutes. Add tomatoes; roast 10 minutes more or until chicken is done (170°F for breasts; 175°F for thighs and drumsticks) and vegetables are tender.

PER SERVING *384 cal., 23 g fat (5 g sat. fat), 104 mg chol., 389 mg sodium, 8 g carb., 2 g fiber, 35 g pro.*

PREP 15 minutes
ROAST 45 minutes

4 servings	ingredients	8 servings
3 Tbsp.	olive oil	6 Tbsp.
2½ tsp.	dried tarragon, thyme, or basil, crushed	5 tsp.
4 cloves	garlic, minced	8 cloves
½ tsp.	salt	1 tsp.
½ tsp.	black pepper	1 tsp.
1 lb.	roma tomatoes, quartered lengthwise	2 lb.
2 small	onions, cut into wedges	4 small
2 lb. (total)	meaty chicken pieces (breast halves, thighs, and/or drumsticks), skin removed if desired	4 lb. (total)

Pesto Chicken Breasts with Zucchini

Bone-in chicken breasts turn out juicier and more flavorful than chicken roasted off the bone. This summery dish has bold flavor from tomato pesto in both the chicken and the zucchini and summer squash serve-along.

1. Preheat oven to 350°F. Loosen the skin on one edge of each chicken breast half. Rub about 2 teaspoons pesto under and over the skin of each breast half. Arrange chicken in a 15×10×1-inch baking pan. Bake 45 to 55 minutes or until chicken is done (170°F). Remove chicken from oven; cover and keep warm.

2. Preheat broiler. Place zucchini and/or yellow squash on the unheated rack of a broiler pan. Brush both sides with oil and sprinkle with salt and pepper. Broil about 4 inches from the heat for 8 to 10 minutes or just until tender, turning once halfway through broiling.

3. Cut squash into ¼-inch slices. In a bowl combine squash, the remaining pesto, and, if desired, hot cooked pasta; toss gently to coat. Serve chicken with squash and, if desired, sprinkle with basil.

PER SERVING *472 cal., 26 g fat (7 g sat. fat), 145 mg chol., 553 mg sodium, 8 g carb., 2 g fiber, 49 g pro.*

PREP **20 minutes**
BAKE **45 minutes**
BROIL **8 minutes**

4 servings	ingredients	8 servings
4 (about 2½ lb. total)	bone-in chicken breast halves	8 (about 5 lb.) total)
½ cup	dried tomato pesto or basil pesto	1 cup
2 medium	zucchini and/or yellow summer squash, trimmed and halved lengthwise	4 medium
1 Tbsp.	olive oil	2 Tbsp.
¼ tsp.	salt	½ tsp.
⅛ tsp.	black pepper	¼ tsp.
	Hot cooked angel hair pasta (optional)	
	Small fresh basil leaves (optional)	

Cashew Chicken Stir-Fry

START TO FINISH 25 minutes

6 servings	ingredients	12 servings
1¼ cups	sliced zucchini	2½ cups
½ cup	sliced carrot	1 cup
½ cup	sliced onion	1 cup
¾ cup	red sweet pepper strips	1½ cups
2½ cups	shredded green cabbage	5 cups
1 Tbsp.	cooking oil or peanut oil	2 Tbsp.
12 oz.	skinless, boneless chicken breast halves, cut into strips	24 oz.
½ cup	bottled stir-fry sauce	1 cup
½ tsp.	ground ginger	1 tsp.
3 to 4 cups	hot cooked white or brown rice	6 to 8 cups
¾ cup	chopped cocktail peanuts or cashews	1½ cups

Stir-fries come together quickly, so be sure to have each ingredient of the recipe chopped, mixed, and ready before you begin cooking.

1. In a large skillet or wok cook half the zucchini, carrot, onion, sweet pepper, and cabbage in hot oil over medium-high heat for 2 minutes or until crisp-tender, stirring occasionally. Remove vegetables from skillet. Cook remaining vegetables; remove from skillet.

2. If necessary, add more oil to skillet. Add chicken; cook and stir for 3 to 5 minutes or until chicken is no longer pink. Push chicken from center of skillet. Add stir-fry sauce and ginger to center of skillet; cook and stir until bubbly. Return vegetables to skillet; cook and stir for 1 minute or until heated through. Serve over rice and sprinkle with chopped peanuts.

PER SERVING *355 cal., 14 g fat (2 g sat. fat), 33 mg chol., 816 mg sodium, 37 g carb., 5 g fiber, 22 g pro.*

Greek Stuffed Chicken and Greens

These stuffed chicken breasts offer a healthy and quick option for busy weeknight dinners. With fresh salad greens and a drizzle of vinaigrette, the meal is light and satisfying.

1. Place tomatoes in a small bowl. Add enough boiling water to cover the tomatoes. Let stand for 10 minutes. Drain and pat dry; set aside.

2. Meanwhile, using a sharp knife, make a pocket in each chicken breast half by cutting horizontally through the thickest portion to, but not through, the opposite side. Set chicken aside.

3. In a small bowl combine feta cheese, cream cheese, the basil, and tomatoes. Spoon about 1 rounded tablespoon into the pocket in each chicken breast half. If necessary, secure openings with wooden toothpicks. Sprinkle chicken with pepper.

4. In a large nonstick skillet heat oil over medium-high heat. Cook chicken in the hot oil for 12 to 14 minutes or until no longer pink (170°F), turning once. (Reduce heat to medium if chicken browns too quickly.) If desired, serve chicken with salad greens and drizzle with reduced-fat vinaigrette.

TIP If desired, for 4 servings, substitute ½ teaspoon dried basil, crushed, for the fresh basil. For 8 servings, substitute 1 teaspoon dried basil, crushed, for the fresh basil.

PER SERVING *173 cal., 6 g fat (2 g sat. fat), 82 mg chol., 265 mg sodium, 1 g carb., 0 g fiber, 27 g pro.*

START TO FINISH **30 minutes**

4 servings	ingredients	8 servings
1 Tbsp.	snipped dried tomatoes (not oil-packed)	2 Tbsp.
4 (1 to 1½ lb. total)	skinless, boneless chicken breast halves	8 (2 to 3 lb. total)
¼ cup	crumbled feta cheese	½ cup
2 Tbsp.	softened fat-free cream cheese	¼ cup
2 tsp.	snipped fresh basil*	4 tsp.
⅛ tsp.	black pepper	¼ tsp.
1 tsp.	olive oil or canola oil	2 tsp.
	Salad greens (optional)	
	Bottled reduced-fat vinaigrette (optional)	

Chicken, Bacon, and Veggie Skillet

Fresh asparagus and summer squash make this lemony braised chicken a one-pan meal. Not a fan of asparagus? Swap it out with fresh green beans for an equally tasty option.

START TO FINISH 45 minutes

4 servings	ingredients	8 servings
1 lb.	asparagus spears trimmed and cut in half, or green beans	2 lb.
4 slices	bacon, coarsely chopped	8 slices
4 (1½ lb. total)	skinless, boneless chicken breast halves	8 (3 lb. total)
	Salt	
	Black pepper	
1 medium	yellow summer squash, halved lengthwise and cut into ½-inch slices	2 medium
one 14.5-oz. can	chicken broth	two 14.5-oz. cans
2 Tbsp.	all-purpose flour	¼ cup
½ tsp.	finely shredded lemon peel	1 tsp.
	Lemon wedges	

1. In a large saucepan cook asparagus in a small amount of boiling water for 3 minutes or until crisp-tender; drain. Immediately plunge into ice water to stop cooking.

2. In a large skillet cook bacon over medium heat until crisp. Using a slotted spoon, remove bacon and drain on paper towels, reserving 1 tablespoon drippings in skillet.

3. Sprinkle chicken with salt and pepper. Cook chicken in reserved drippings over medium-high heat for 12 minutes, turning once. Remove chicken from skillet; keep warm.

4. Add squash to skillet; cook 3 minutes, stirring occasionally. In a medium bowl whisk together broth, flour, and lemon peel; add to squash in skillet. Cook and stir until thickened and bubbly. Stir in asparagus and chicken. Cook 6 minutes or until chicken is done (170°F). Sprinkle with bacon. Serve with lemon wedges.

FOR 8 SERVINGS In Step 2 reserve 2 tablespoons drippings in skillet.

PER SERVING *272 cal., 11 g fat (3 g sat. fat), 105 mg chol., 891 mg sodium, 8 g carb., 2 g fiber, 36 g pro.*

Chicken with Parmesan Noodles

From skillet to plate in just 20 minutes, this updated version of chicken and noodles gets extra flavor from basil pesto.

1. Cook pasta according to package directions.

2. Meanwhile, in an extra-large skillet heat half the butter over medium heat. Add carrots; cook 3 minutes. Add chicken; cook and stir for 4 to 5 minutes or until chicken is no longer pink. Add 4 tablespoons of the pesto; toss to coat.

3. Drain pasta. Return to hot pan; toss with the remaining butter and remaining pesto. Serve with chicken. Sprinkle pasta with Parmesan cheese. If desired, drizzle with olive oil and top with basil.

FOR 12 SERVINGS In Step 2 use 8 tablespoons pesto.

PER SERVING *390 cal., 16 g fat (5 g sat. fat), 114 mg chol., 369 mg sodium, 28 g carb., 3 g fiber, 33 g pro.*

START TO FINISH **20 minutes**

6 servings	ingredients	12 servings
one 9-oz. pkg.	refrigerated angel hair pasta	two 9-oz. pkg.
2 Tbsp.	butter	¼ cup
2 cups	thinly sliced carrots	4 cups
1½ lb.	skinless, boneless chicken breast halves, cut into pieces	3 lb.
6 Tbsp.	basil pesto	¾ cup
¼ cup	finely shredded Parmesan cheese	½ cup
	Olive oil (optional)	
	Fresh basil (optional)	

Lemon-Thyme Roasted Chicken with Fingerlings

Eating healthfully doesn't mean skimping on flavor. By adding the entire lemon—peel, rind, and all—to the skillet, you double the citrus flavor while keeping the fat and calories low.

1. In an extra-large skillet heat half the oil over medium heat. Stir in half the dried thyme, the salt, and pepper. Add potatoes; toss gently to coat. Cook, covered, for 12 minutes, stirring twice.

2. Stir potatoes; push to one side of skillet. Add the remaining oil to opposite side of skillet. Arrange chicken in skillet alongside potatoes. Cook, uncovered, for 5 minutes.

3. Turn chicken. Sprinkle with garlic and the remaining dried thyme; top with lemon slices. Cook, covered, for 7 to 10 minutes more or until chicken is no longer pink (170°F) and potatoes are tender. If desired, sprinkle with fresh thyme.

PER SERVING *255 cal., 6 g fat (1 g sat. fat), 66 mg chol., 307 mg sodium, 21 g carb., 3 g fiber, 29 g pro.*

START TO FINISH **30 minutes**

4 servings	ingredients	8 servings
4 tsp.	canola oil or olive oil	3 Tbs.
1 tsp.	dried thyme, crushed	2 tsp.
¼ tsp.	salt	½ tsp.
¼ tsp.	freshly ground black pepper	½ tsp.
1 lb.	fingerling potatoes, halved lengthwise, and/or tiny new red or white potatoes, halved	2 lb.
4 (1 to 1¼ lb. total)	skinless, boneless chicken breast halves	8 (2 to 2½ lb. total)
2 cloves	garlic, minced	4 cloves
1	lemon, thinly sliced	2
	Snipped fresh thyme (optional)	

Chicken, Macaroni, and Cheese

Herbed semisoft cheese gives this lightened skillet version of mac and cheese plenty of flavor. Find the cheese with other specialty cheeses.

START TO FINISH 35 minutes

5 servings	ingredients	10 servings
6 oz.	dried regular or multigrain elbow macaroni	12 oz.
	Nonstick cooking spray	
12 oz.	skinless, boneless chicken breast halves, cut into 1-inch pieces	24 oz.
¼ cup	finely chopped onion	½ cup
one 6.5-oz. pkg.	light semisoft cheese with garlic and fines herbes	two 6.5-oz. pkg.
1⅔ cups	fat-free milk	3⅓ cups
1 Tbsp.	all-purpose flour	2 Tbsp.
¾ cup	shredded reduced-fat cheddar cheese	1½ cups
2 cups	fresh baby spinach	4 cups
1 cup	grape or cherry tomatoes, quartered	2 cups

1. Cook macaroni according to package directions, except do not add salt to the water; drain.

2. Meanwhile, coat a large nonstick skillet with cooking spray; heat skillet over medium-high heat. Add chicken and onion; cook 4 to 6 minutes or until chicken is no longer pink and onion is tender, stirring frequently. (If onion browns too quickly, reduce heat to medium.) Remove from heat. Stir in semisoft cheese until melted.

3. In a medium bowl whisk together milk and flour until smooth. Gradually stir milk mixture into chicken mixture. Cook and stir over medium heat until thickened and bubbly. Reduce heat to low. Gradually add cheddar cheese, stirring until melted. Add cooked macaroni; cook and stir for 1 to 2 minutes or until heated through. Stir in spinach. Top with cherry tomatoes. Serve immediately.

PER SERVING *369 cal., 12 g fat (7 g sat. fat), 85 mg chol., 393 mg sodium, 33 g carb., 4 g fiber, 33 g pro.*

PREP 15 minutes
STAND 1 hour
GRILL 12 minutes

Chicken Salad with Grapes

Ideal for easy summer meals, this salad is drizzled with a make-ahead balsamic vinaigrette dressing.

1. For vinaigrette, in a screw-top jar combine oil, vinegar, dill, oregano, mustard, pepper, and garlic. Cover and shake well. Let stand for 1 hour before using.

2. Meanwhile, sprinkle chicken lightly with steak seasoning. Grill chicken, covered, over medium heat for 12 to 15 minutes or until no longer pink (170°F), turning once. Cool slightly. Slice chicken.

3. Arrange greens on serving plates. Add sliced chicken, grapes, cheese, and pine nuts. Shake vinaigrette; drizzle over salads.

*TIP If desired, for 4 servings substitute 2 teaspoons dried dill, crushed, in place of fresh dill, and ¼ teaspoon dried oregano, crushed, for the fresh. For 8 servings, use 4 teaspoons dried dill, crushed, in place of fresh dill, and ½ teaspoon dried oregano in place of the fresh oregano.

PER SERVING 464 cal., 29 g fat (6 g sat. fat), 105 mg chol., 317 mg sodium, 13 g carb., 3 g fiber, 38 g pro.

4 servings	ingredients	8 servings
¼ cup	olive oil	½ cup
3 Tbsp.	balsamic vinegar	6 Tbsp.
2 Tbsp.	snipped fresh dill*	¼ cup
½ tsp.	snipped fresh oregano*	1 tsp.
½ tsp.	dry mustard	1 tsp.
¼ tsp.	black pepper	½ tsp.
1 clove	garlic, minced	2 cloves
4 (1¼ to 1½ lb. total)	skinless, boneless chicken breast halves	8 (2½ to 3 lb. total)
	Montreal or Kansas City steak seasoning	
8 cups	mixed greens	16 cups
¾ cup	seedless red grapes, halved	1½ cups
⅓ cup	crumbled goat cheese (chèvre)	⅔ cup
¼ cup	pine nuts, toasted (tip, page 12)	½ cup

Ginger-Lime Chicken Sandwiches

Fresh ginger in the marinade gives the chicken gentle warmth that balances tangy lime juice. If you don't use ginger often, store it in the freezer, then grate the frozen root as needed.

1. Cut chicken in half horizontally. Sprinkle with salt and pepper. Place chicken in a resealable plastic bag set in a shallow dish.

2. For marinade, in a medium bowl whisk together cilantro, lime peel, lime juice, oil, honey, and ginger. Pour marinade over chicken. Seal bag; turn to coat chicken. Marinate in the refrigerator for 1 to 4 hours, turning bag occasionally.

3. Meanwhile, for garlic mayonnaise, in a small bowl combine mayonnaise and garlic. Cover and chill until needed.

4. Drain chicken, discarding marinade. Grill chicken, covered, over medium heat for 7 to 8 minutes or until no longer pink (170°F), turning once.

5. Layer bottoms of buns with lettuce, chicken, and red onion. Spread tops of buns with garlic mayonnaise.

PER SERVING *422 cal., 24 g fat (4 g sat. fat), 60 mg chol., 698 mg sodium, 28 g carb., 1 g fiber, 23 g pro.*

PREP **20 minutes**
MARINATE **1 hour**
GRILL **7 minutes**

4 servings	ingredients	8 servings
two 6-oz.	skinless, boneless chicken breast halves	four 6-oz.
½ tsp.	coarse salt	1 tsp.
¼ tsp.	freshly ground black pepper	½ tsp.
¼ cup	snipped fresh cilantro	½ cup
2 tsp.	finely shredded lime peel	4 tsp.
3 Tbsp.	lime juice	6 Tbsp.
2 Tbsp.	olive oil	¼ cup
2 Tbsp.	honey	¼ cup
1 to 2 Tbsp.	grated fresh ginger	2 to 4 Tbsp.
¼ cup	mayonnaise	½ cup
2 cloves	garlic, minced	4 cloves
4	hamburger buns or kaiser rolls, split and toasted	8
4	lettuce leaves	8
	Thinly sliced red onion	

Mediterranean Pizza Skillet

When you don't have bread on hand, serve this pizza-inspired chicken and vegetable mix over pasta, couscous, or mixed greens.

1. In a large skillet heat oil over medium-high heat. Add chicken and garlic; cook and stir for 2 to 4 minutes or until chicken is browned. Stir in artichoke hearts, tomatoes, olives, Italian seasoning, and pepper.

2. Bring to boiling; reduce heat. Simmer, covered, 10 minutes or until chicken is no longer pink. Top with lettuce and cheese. Cook, covered, for 1 to 2 minutes more or just until lettuce begins to wilt. Sprinkle with basil. Serve on or with toasted bread slices.

PER SERVING *395 cal., 17 g fat (6 g sat. fat), 82 mg chol., 1,003 mg sodium, 27 g carb., 6 g fiber, 33 g pro.*

START TO FINISH **30 minutes**

4 servings	ingredients	8 servings
2 Tbsp.	olive oil	¼ cup
1 lb.	skinless, boneless chicken breast halves, cut into ¾-inch pieces	2 lb.
2 cloves	garlic, minced	4 cloves
one 14-oz. can	quartered artichoke hearts, drained	two 14-oz. cans
1⅓ cups	chopped roma tomatoes	2⅔ cups
one 2.25-oz. can	sliced pitted ripe olives, drained	two 2.25-oz. cans
½ tsp.	dried Italian seasoning, crushed	1 tsp.
¼ tsp.	black pepper	½ tsp.
2 cups	romaine lettuce or mesclun, shredded	4 cups
1 cup	crumbled feta cheese	2 cups
⅓ cup	fresh basil leaves, shredded	⅔ cup
	Crusty Italian or French bread slices, toasted	

Chicken, Bacon, and Cheddar Submarines

Assemble and chill these chicken sandwiches for a next-day picnic or potluck.

1. Sprinkle chicken with garlic salt and pepper. Brush both sides of onion slices with oil. Grill chicken and onion, covered, over medium heat for 12 to 15 minutes or until chicken is no longer pink (170°F) and onion is tender and lightly charred, turning once. Remove from grill. Thinly slice chicken. Separate onion into rings.

2. Meanwhile, preheat oven to 400°F. Line a 15×10×1-inch baking pan with foil. Place bacon on the prepared baking pan. Bake 15 minutes or until bacon is crisp (no need to turn bacon). Remove from pan and drain on paper towels.

3. In a small bowl combine mayonnaise and mustard. Cut bread loaves in half horizontally. Spread the insides of bread halves with mayonnaise-mustard. Layer bottom halves with chicken, onion, bacon, and cheese. Replace tops; press down firmly. Tightly wrap each sandwich in foil and chill 8 hours or overnight.

4. Grill foil-wrapped sandwiches, covered, over medium heat for 10 minutes or until heated through, turning every 2 minutes. To serve, cut each sandwich into four portions.

PER SERVING *623 cal., 25 g fat (9 g sat. fat), 67 mg chol., 1,272 mg sodium, 65 g carb., 3 g fiber, 34 g pro.*

PREP 25 minutes
GRILL 22 minutes
BAKE 15 minutes
CHILL 8 hours

4 servings	ingredients	8 servings
6 oz.	skinless, boneless chicken breast halves	12 oz.
⅛ tsp.	garlic salt	¼ tsp.
⅛ tsp.	black pepper	¼ tsp.
½ small	red onion, cut in ½-inch slices	1 small
1½ tsp.	olive oil	1 Tbsp.
4 slices	bacon	8 slices
3 Tbsp.	mayonnaise	⅓ cup
1½ tsp.	coarse ground mustard	1 Tbsp.
one 12-inch loaf	baguette-style French bread	two 12-inch loaves
4 slices	cheddar cheese	8 slices

Chicken and Cauliflower Orecchiette

Orecchiette means "little ears" in Italian. If you can't find this pasta shape, substitute penne, rotini, or shell-shape pasta.

1. Cook pasta according to package directions; drain pasta, reserving ¾ cup cooking water. In an extra-large skillet heat oil over medium heat; add cauliflower and salt, stirring to coat. Cook 8 minutes or until tender and lightly browned, stirring occasionally.

2. Uncover skillet and add chicken and raisins. Cook and stir for 2 to 3 minutes or until heated through. Add pasta and the reserved cooking water to skillet; cook and stir until heated through. Remove from heat. Stir in arugula; top with hazelnuts and shaved Parmesan.

* To toast hazelnuts, preheat oven to 350°F. Spread nuts in a single layer in a shallow baking pan. Bake 8 to 10 minutes or until lightly toasted, stirring once to toast evenly. Cool nuts slightly. Place warm nuts on a clean kitchen towel; rub with the towel to remove loose skins.

FOR 8 SERVINGS In Step 1 reserve 1½ cups cooking water.

PER SERVING *350 cal., 15 g fat (3 g sat. fat), 62 mg chol., 363 mg sodium, 35 g carb., 3 g fiber, 22 g pro.*

START TO FINISH **35 minutes**

4 servings	ingredients	8 servings
4 oz. (1¼ cups)	dried orecchiette pasta	8 oz. (2½ cups)
4 tsp.	olive oil	3 Tbsp.
½ small	head orange, purple, or white cauliflower, cored and chopped	1 small
⅛ tsp.	kosher salt	¼ tsp.
1½ cups	shredded rotisserie chicken	3 cups
¼ cup	golden raisins	½ cup
1½ cups	baby arugula	3 cups
¼ cup	hazelnuts (filberts), toasted* and coarsely chopped	½ cup
	Shaved Parmesan cheese	

Quick Chicken Paella

Be sure to purchase Spanish-style chorizo for this quick, special main dish. Unlike Mexican chorizo—which is raw—the Spanish version of this sausage has been smoked and cooked through.

1. Thaw shrimp, if frozen. Peel and devein shrimp. Rinse shrimp; pat dry with paper towels. Set shrimp aside. In an extra-large skillet heat oil over medium heat. Add chorizo, onion, and garlic to skillet. Cook 5 minutes, stirring occasionally. Add tomatoes, broth, and saffron to skillet. Bring to boiling; stir in the couscous. Reduce heat. Simmer, covered, for 5 minutes.

2. Add shrimp, chicken, and peas to skillet; cover and cook for 5 minutes or until shrimp are opaque and couscous is tender. To serve, sprinkle with parsley.

PER SERVING *455 cal., 19 g fat (6 g sat. fat), 182 mg chol., 1,054 mg sodium, 32 g carb., 4 g fiber, 40 g pro.*

START TO FINISH **30 minutes**

4 servings	ingredients	8 servings
8 oz.	fresh or frozen medium shrimp	16 oz.
1 Tbsp.	olive oil	2 Tbsp.
4 oz.	thinly sliced cooked, smoked chorizo	8 oz.
1 cup	chopped onion	2 cups
2 cloves	garlic, minced	4 cloves
one 14.5-oz. can	diced tomatoes, undrained	two 14.5-oz. cans
one 14.5-oz. can	chicken broth	two 14.5-oz. cans
Dash	saffron threads	⅛ tsp.
¾ cup	Israeli couscous	1½ cups
2 cups	shredded rotisserie chicken	4 cups
½ cup	frozen peas	1 cup
	Snipped fresh Italian parsley	

Spicy Peanut-Chicken Noodles

These Thai-style noodles come together in a snap. To tame the heat of the serrano pepper seed it before adding it to the skillet.

START TO FINISH 30 minutes

6 servings	ingredients	12 servings
6 oz.	pad thai-style brown rice noodles	12 oz.
¼ cup	vegetable oil	½ cup
¾ cup	peanuts, coarsely chopped	1½ cups
1	fresh serrano chile pepper, thinly sliced (tip, page 11)	2
3 cups	shredded rotisserie chicken	6 cups
2 cups	packaged fresh julienned carrots or coarsely shredded fresh carrots	4 cups
½ cup	rice vinegar	1 cup
2 Tbsp.	fish sauce	¼ cup
2 tsp.	sugar	4 tsp.
¼ cup	snipped fresh mint or basil	½ cup
	Lime wedges	
	Snipped fresh mint	

1. Bring a large pot of water to boiling; turn off heat and add rice noodles. Let stand for 5 to 6 minutes or until noodles are softened but not mushy; drain and rinse with cold water. Drain well then transfer to a large bowl; set aside.

2. In an extra-large skillet heat oil over medium heat. Add peanuts and chile pepper to hot oil; cook about 5 minutes or until aromatic and chile slices just begin to brown, stirring frequently. Remove from heat; add shredded chicken and carrots, stirring until no longer sizzling.

3. In a small bowl combine rice vinegar, fish sauce, and sugar; pour over the noodles. Add chicken mixture and mint; toss to coat. Serve with lime wedges and additional fresh mint.

PER SERVING *414 cal., 23 g fat (4 g sat. fat), 63 mg chol., 784 mg sodium, 31 g carb., 5 g fiber, 23 g pro.*

Thai Chicken Noodle Salad

Take 20 minutes to toss this Asian-style salad together in the morning and it will be ready to serve at dinnertime.

1. Remove and discard skin and bones from chicken. Cut chicken into strips. In a medium saucepan bring the water to boiling. Break up each package of ramen noodles (discard seasoning packets or save for another use). Add noodles to boiling water; remove from heat. Cover and let stand for 5 minutes; drain. Rinse with cold water; drain again.

2. Meanwhile, in a large bowl whisk together peanut butter, coconut milk, cilantro, lime juice, and cayenne pepper until smooth. Stir in chicken, cucumber, and green onions. Add noodles; toss to combine. Serve immediately or cover and chill up to 24 hours. Before serving, sprinkle with cashews.

PER SERVING *551 cal., 28 g fat (8 g sat. fat), 113 mg chol., 728 mg sodium, 36 g carb., 4 g fiber, 40 g pro.*

PREP 20 minutes
STAND 5 minutes

6 servings	ingredients	12 servings
one 2¼- to 2½-lb.	rotisserie chicken	two 2¼- to 2½-lb.
4 cups	water	8 cups
two 3-oz. pkg.	ramen noodles	four 3-oz. pkg.
¾ cup	reduced-fat creamy peanut butter	1½ cups
¾ cup	unsweetened light coconut milk	1½ cups
¼ cup	snipped fresh cilantro	½ cup
¼ cup	lime juice	½ cup
¼ tsp.	cayenne pepper	½ tsp.
1 small	seedless cucumber, halved lengthwise and cut into ¼-inch pieces	2 small
6	green onions, thinly sliced	12
¼ cup	chopped cashews	½ cup

Chicken Jambalaya Skillet

Cubed butternut squash sweet complements spicy andouille sausage in this healthful, fast take on jambalaya.

1. In a large nonstick skillet heat oil over medium heat. Add sausage; cook until lightly browned, stirring occasionally. Stir in squash, beans, sweet pepper, broth, celery, onion, the water, tomato paste, bay leaf, thyme, and allspice.

2. Bring to boiling; reduce heat. Simmer, covered, for 10 minutes. Simmer, uncovered, for 5 minutes more or until jambalaya is slightly thickened. Remove and discard bay leaf. Serve jambalaya over rice. If desired, sprinkle with additional thyme.

*TIP If desired, for 5 servings, substitute 1 teaspoon dried thyme, crushed, for fresh thyme. For 10 servings, substitute 2 teaspoons dried thyme, crushed, for the fresh thyme.

PER SERVING *272 cal., 6 g fat (1 g sat. fat), 35 mg chol., 626 mg sodium, 41 g carb., 8 g fiber, 16 g pro.*

PREP 25 minutes
COOK 15 minutes

5 servings	ingredients	10 servings
1 tsp.	canola oil	2 tsp.
8 oz.	smoked chicken andouille sausage, cut diagonally into ½-inch slices	16 oz.
2 cups	cubed butternut squash	4 cups
one 15-oz. can	red kidney beans, rinsed and drained	two 15-oz. cans
1 cup	chopped green sweet pepper	2 cups
1 cup	reduced-sodium chicken broth	2 cups
¾ cup	chopped celery	1½ cups
¾ cup	chopped onion	1½ cups
¾ cup	water	1½ cups
¼ cup	no-salt-added tomato paste	½ cup
1	bay leaf	2
1 Tbsp.	snipped fresh thyme*	2 Tbsp.
⅛ tsp.	ground allspice	¼ tsp.
1⅔ cups	hot cooked brown rice	3⅓ cups

Fast Pho

Pronounced FUH, this quick-to-make version of the traditional slow-simmered Vietnamese soup gets its signature flavor from cinnamon, ginger, star anise, and a squeeze of fresh lime juice.

1. Cook noodles according to package directions; drain.

2. Meanwhile, in a large saucepan combine broth, fish sauce, cinnamon sticks, ginger, and, if desired, star anise. Bring to boiling; reduce heat. Simmer, covered, 5 minutes. Add green onions; simmer, uncovered, 5 minutes. Add chicken; simmer, uncovered, 1 minute more. Remove and discard cinnamon sticks and star anise.

3. Divide cooked noodles among soup bowls. Ladle broth over noodles. Serve with herbs and lime wedges, and, if desired, bok choy and jalapeño.

PER SERVING *310 cal., 6 g fat (2 g sat. fat), 62 mg chol., 900 mg sodium, 38 g carb., 4 g fiber, 24 g pro.*

START TO FINISH **30 minutes**

4 servings	ingredients	8 servings
6 oz.	brown-rice or regular banh pho (Vietnamese wide rice noodles)	12 oz.
3½ cups	low sodium vegetable broth or reduced-sodium chicken broth	7 cups
2 Tbsp.	fish sauce or reduced-sodium soy sauce	¼ cup
one 4-inch	stick cinnamon	two 4-inch
one 1-inch piece	fresh ginger, sliced and cut into strips	two 1-inch pieces
1	star anise (optional)	2
3	green onions, trimmed and cut into thin 1-inch strips	6
2 cups	cubed cooked chicken, thinly sliced cooked pork, or cooked shrimp	4 cups
½ cup	fresh basil, cilantro, and/or mint leaves	1 cup
	Lime wedges	
2 cups	shredded bok choy or bean sprouts (optional)	4 cups
	Sliced fresh jalapeño (tip, page 11) or Asian chili sauce (sriracha sauce) (optional)	

Moroccan Skillet Turkey

Salsa gives this 30-minute skillet extra flavor in just one ingredient. Raisins and honey provide subtle sweetness.

1. In a large skillet heat oil over medium-high heat. Add turkey; cook 4 minutes or until browned, turning once. In a medium bowl combine salsa, raisins, honey, cumin, and cinnamon; stir into turkey. Bring to boiling; reduce heat. Simmer, covered, for 10 to 12 minutes or until turkey is no longer pink (170°F).

2. Meanwhile, in a medium saucepan bring the water and salt to boiling. Stir in couscous. Remove from heat. Cover and let stand for 5 minutes.

3. Fluff couscous with a fork. Serve turkey over couscous. Sprinkle with almonds and parsley.

PER SERVING *447 cal., 8 g fat (1 g sat. fat), 105 mg chol., 598 mg sodium, 44 g carb., 4 g fiber, 49 g pro.*

START TO FINISH **30 minutes**

4 servings	ingredients	8 servings
1 Tbsp.	olive oil	2 Tbsp.
2	turkey breast tenderloins, halved horizontally	4
1 cup	salsa	2 cups
¼ cup	raisins	½ cup
1 Tbsp.	honey	2 Tbsp.
½ tsp.	ground cumin	1 tsp.
¼ tsp.	ground cinnamon	½ tsp.
1 cup	water	2 cups
¼ tsp.	salt	½ tsp.
¾ cup	couscous	1½ cups
¼ cup	slivered almonds, toasted (tip, page 12)	½ cup
	Snipped fresh Italian parsley	

Sloppy Turkey and Chili Joes

4 servings	ingredients	8 servings
1 to 1¼ lb.	ground turkey breast	2 to 2½ lb.
½ cup	chopped onion	1 cup
1 medium	fresh poblano chile pepper, seeded and chopped (tip, page 11)	2 medium
one 15-oz. can	tomato sauce	two 15-oz. cans
2 Tbsp.	packed brown sugar	¼ cup
1 Tbsp.	Worcestershire sauce	2 Tbsp.
2 tsp.	chili powder	4 tsp.
½ tsp.	garlic powder	1 tsp.
	Salt and black pepper	
4	kaiser rolls, split and toasted	8
	Fresh basil leaves (optional)	
4	slices Monterey Jack cheese	8
	Green and/or red sweet pepper rings (optional)	
	Thinly sliced tomato (optional)	
	Thinly sliced onion (optional)	

Serve these Southwest-style sloppy joes to kids. They'll love building their own sandwiches, the sweet-savory sauce, and the variety of toppings.

1. In a large nonstick skillet cook ground turkey, onion, and chile pepper over medium heat until turkey is no longer pink. Stir in tomato sauce, brown sugar, Worcestershire sauce, chili powder, and garlic powder. Bring to boiling; reduce heat. Simmer, covered, for 15 minutes, stirring occasionally. Season to taste with salt and black pepper.

2. Place roll bottoms on dinner plates; if desired, top with basil leaves. Add cheese slices then top with turkey joes. If desired, top with sweet pepper, tomato, and/or onion.

PER SERVING *470 cal., 10 g fat (5 g sat. fat), 84 mg chol., 1,119 mg sodium, 53 g carb., 3 g fiber, 41 g pro.*

Spicy Stir-Fried Turkey and Greens

Curry powder—a blend of up to 20 spices, including bright yellow turmeric—gives this stir-fry Middle East flavor and color.

1. In a large skillet or wok heat oil over medium-high heat. Add sweet peppers and onion; cook and stir for 3 minutes. Add garlic; cook and stir for 1 minute more. Remove from skillet.

2. Add ground turkey, curry powder, ginger, salt, and black pepper to hot skillet. Cook and stir for 5 minutes or until turkey is no longer pink, using a wooden spoon to break up turkey as it cooks.

3. Add spinach and the water to turkey in skillet; return vegetables. Cook and stir just until spinach is wilted. Stir in yogurt. Serve stir-fry over hot cooked couscous. If desired, sprinkle with almonds.

PER SERVING *479 cal., 19 g fat (5 g sat. fat), 91 mg chol., 426 mg sodium, 48 g carb., 5 g fiber, 29 g pro.*

START TO FINISH **30 minutes**

4 servings	ingredients	8 servings
1 Tbsp.	canola oil or vegetable oil	2 Tbsp.
2 medium	red sweet peppers, seeded and cut into 1-inch pieces	4 medium
1 small	onion, cut into ½-inch-thick wedges	2 small
2 cloves	garlic, minced	4 cloves
1 lb.	ground turkey	2 lb.
2 tsp.	curry powder	4 tsp.
one 1-inch piece	fresh ginger, grated	two 1-inch pieces
½ tsp.	salt	1 tsp.
½ tsp.	freshly ground black pepper	1 tsp.
6 cups	fresh spinach leaves	12 cups
3 Tbsp.	water	6 Tbsp.
one 6-oz. carton	plain low-fat yogurt	two 6-oz. cartons
4 cups	hot cooked couscous	8 cups
	Sliced almonds, toasted (tip, page 12) (optional)	

Turkey Panini with Pesto-Mayo

A simple yet flavorful mix of mayo and pesto makes these Italian-style pressed sandwiches special. If you're not a fan of sourdough, use Italian-style bread.

1. In a small bowl combine mayonnaise and pesto. Spread bread slices with pesto-mayo. Layer turkey, pepperoni, and roasted pepper on four of the bread slices; add cheese. Top with remaining bread. Lightly brush outside of sandwiches with oil.

2. Preheat a covered indoor grill, panini press, grill pan, or large skillet. Place sandwiches, half at a time if necessary, in grill or panini press. Cover and cook 6 to 8 minutes or until golden brown and cheese is melted. (If using a grill pan or skillet, place sandwiches on grill pan or skillet. Weight sandwiches with a heavy skillet and cook 2 minutes. Turn sandwiches over, weight, and cook 2 to 3 minutes more or until golden brown and cheese is melted.)

PER SERVING *506 cal., 30 g fat (11 g sat. fat), 80 mg chol., 1,534 mg sodium, 30 g carb., 2 g fiber, 29 g pro.*

START TO FINISH **30 minutes**

4 servings	ingredients	8 servings
2 Tbsp.	mayonnaise or salad dressing	¼ cup
1 Tbsp.	basil pesto	2 Tbsp.
8	slices sourdough bread	16
8 oz.	thinly sliced cooked turkey breast	16 oz.
one 3.5-oz. pkg.	thinly sliced pepperoni	two 3.5-oz. pkg.
½ cup	sliced roasted red sweet pepper	1 cup
4 oz.	sliced provolone cheese	8 oz.
1 to 2 Tbsp.	olive oil	2 to 4 Tbsp.

CHAPTER 3

Meat

Build easy, nutritious meals around beef, pork, lamb, or bison and you will be sure to satisfy big appetites any night of the week.

77

82

101

Lamb Chops with Grape-Balsamic Sauce

Reserved for special dinners, these rosemary-seasoned chops are finished in a simple pan sauce of tangy balsamic vinegar and sweet grapes. Complete the meal with mashed potatoes and asparagus.

1. Trim fat from chops. In a small bowl combine rosemary, salt, and pepper. Sprinkle over chops; rub in with your fingers.

2. In a large nonstick skillet heat oil over medium heat. Add lamb chops. Cook 8 to 10 minutes or until lamb is desired doneness (145°F for medium rare or 160°F for medium), turning once. Remove chops from skillet. Keep warm.

3. For grape-balsamic sauce, in the same skillet combine grapes, vinegar, and the water. Cook and stir just until boiling; reduce heat. Cook and stir for 1 to 2 minutes more or until grapes are softened but still hold their shape. Serve sauce with chops. If desired, sprinkle with fresh mint.

*TIP If desired, for 2 servings substitute two 4-ounce boneless pork loin chops, cut ¾ inch thick, for the lamb chops. For 4 servings, substitute four 4-ounce boneless pork loin chops, cut ¾ inch thick, for the lamb chops. Cook pork 8 to 10 minutes or until slightly pink in the center (145°F), turning once.

PER SERVING *230 cal., 10 g fat (3 g sat. fat), 75 mg chol., 205 mg sodium, 10 g carb., 0 g fiber, 24 g pro.*

START TO FINISH **20 minutes**

2 servings	ingredients	4 servings
4 (10 to 12 oz. total)	small lamb rib chops*	8 (20 to 24 oz. total)
1 tsp.	snipped fresh rosemary	2 tsp.
⅛ tsp.	salt	¼ tsp.
⅛ tsp.	black pepper	¼ tsp.
2 tsp.	olive oil	4 tsp.
1 cup	seedless red grapes, halved	2 cups
1 Tbsp.	balsamic vinegar	2 Tbsp.
1 Tbsp.	water	2 Tbsp.
1 Tbsp.	snipped fresh mint (optional)	2 Tbsp.

Bison-Zucchini Burgers

Sauteed zucchini and onion ensure these extra-lean bison burgers remain moist after cooking. If bison isn't available, substitute lean ground beef.

1. In a large skillet heat oil over medium-high heat. Add chopped zucchini and chopped onion; cook 5 to 8 minutes or until vegetables are tender, stirring occasionally. Cool.

2. In a large bowl combine egg, bread crumbs, Parmesan cheese, basil, salt, and pepper. Add zucchini mixture and ground bison; mix gently. Shape into eight ¾-inch-thick patties.

3. Grill patties, covered, over medium heat for 14 to 18 minutes or until patties are done (160°F), turning once halfway through grilling.

4. Serve patties on buns spread with mustard. If desired, top with red onion slices and zucchini ribbons.

*TIP If desired, for 4 servings, use 1½ teaspoons dried basil, crushed, for the fresh oregano. For 8 servings, use 1 tablespoon dried oregano, crushed, for the fresh oregano.

**TIP Trim the ends of two small zucchini. Using a vegetable peeler, cut the squash lengthwise into thin ribbons. Toss the zucchini ribbons with red onion slices and a little red wine vinegar, olive oil, salt, and pepper.

PER SERVING *362 cal., 14 g fat (5 g sat. fat), 113 mg chol., 542 mg sodium, 27 g carb., 3 g fiber, 31 g pro.*

PREP **20 minutes**
GRILL **14 minutes**

4 servings	ingredients	8 servings
1½ tsp.	olive oil	1 Tbsp.
½ cup	finely chopped zucchini	1 cup
½ cup	finely chopped red or yellow onion	1 cup
1	eggs, lightly beaten	2
½ cup	soft bread crumbs	1 cup
¼ cup	grated Parmesan cheese	½ cup
1 Tbsp.	snipped fresh basil*	2 Tbsp.
¼ tsp.	salt	½ tsp.
¼ tsp.	black pepper	½ tsp.
1 lb.	ground bison or lean ground beef	2 lb.
4	whole grain hamburger buns or sandwich rolls, split and, if desired, toasted	8
	Whole grain mustard	
	Red onion slices and zucchini ribbons (optional)**	

Bison Steaks with Grilled Balsamic-Honey Peaches

PREP 20 minutes
GRILL 15 minutes

4 servings	ingredients	8 servings
3 cups	sliced peaches	6 cups
2 Tbsp.	honey	¼ cup
2 Tbsp.	balsamic vinegar	¼ cup
1 Tbsp.	packed brown sugar	2 Tbsp.
1 tsp.	finely chopped crystallized ginger	2 tsp.
four 10-oz.	boneless bison top loin steaks, cut 1 inch thick	eight 10-oz.
1 Tbsp.	cracked black pepper	2 Tbsp.
¾ tsp.	salt or kosher salt	1½ tsp.

Honey- and balsamic vinegar-glazed peaches are grilled alongside the steaks. The peaches would also taste amazing spooned over grilled pork chops or other steaks.

1. Fold a 36×18-inch sheet of heavy foil in half to an 18-inch square. Place peach slices in the center of foil. In a small bowl combine honey, vinegar, brown sugar, and ginger; drizzle over peaches. Bring up opposite edges of foil; seal with a double fold. Fold in remaining ends to completely enclose peaches, leaving space for steam to build.

2. Trim fat from steaks. Sprinkle steaks with pepper and salt; rub in with your fingers.

3. Grill steaks and foil packets, covered, over medium heat until steaks reach desired doneness and peaches are tender, turning once. For steaks, allow 14 to 18 minutes for medium rare (145°F) or 18 to 22 minutes for medium (160°F). For peaches, allow 15 to 20 minutes. Serve steaks with grilled peach slices.

PER SERVING *437 cal., 7 g fat (3 g sat. fat), 201 mg chol., 588 mg sodium, 29 g carb., 2 g fiber, 62 g pro.*

Greek Burgers

These dressed-up Greek-style patties offer an enticing change from traditional burgers. Using a heavy skillet—such as cast-iron—to cook them is essential for browning and caramelizing.

1. In a large bowl combine half the fresh or dried oregano, the Worcestershire sauce, salt, and black pepper. Add ground beef; mix well. Shape into four ½-inch-thick patties; set aside.

2. In a large cast-iron or other heavy skillet heat half the oil over medium-high heat. Add mushrooms, sweet pepper, and onions; cook 4 to 5 minutes or until crisp-tender, stirring occasionally. Remove from heat. Stir in remaining oregano. Remove vegetables from skillet; cover and keep warm.

3. Add remaining oil to skillet; heat over medium-high heat; add patties. Cook 12 to 15 minutes or until a thermometer registers 160°F, turning once.

4. Layer toasted rolls with patties, vegetables, and cheese.

*TIP If desired, for 4 servings, use 1 teaspoon dried oregano, crushed, for the fresh oregano. For 8 servings, use 2 teaspoons dried oregano, crushed, for the fresh oregano.

PER SERVING *652 cal., 37 g fat (13 g sat. fat), 126 mg chol., 840 mg sodium, 37 g carb., 3 g fiber, 41 g pro.*

PREP **20 minutes**
COOK **16 minutes**

4 servings	ingredients	8 servings
1 Tbsp.	snipped fresh oregano*	2 Tbsp.
2 tsp.	Worcestershire sauce	4 tsp.
½ tsp.	kosher salt	1 tsp.
¼ tsp.	freshly ground black pepper	½ tsp.
1½ lb.	ground beef sirloin	3 lb.
2 Tbsp.	olive oil	¼ cup
1½ cups	thickly sliced fresh button or cremini mushrooms	3 cups
1 cup	red sweet pepper strips	2 cups
2	small red onions, sliced	4
4	kaiser rolls, split and toasted	8
⅓ cup	crumbled feta cheese	⅔ cup

Quick Skillet Lasagna

This five-ingredient, 30-minute pasta skillet is an ideal dinner choice for busy weeknights. Top with fresh basil or parsley if you have it on hand.

1. Cook pasta according to package directions; drain. Meanwhile, in a large nonstick skillet cook ground beef over medium-high heat until browned. Remove meat from skillet. Wipe out skillet with a paper towel.

2. Spread about half the cooked pasta in the skillet. Top with about half the sauce. Spoon cooked meat over sauce; sprinkle with two-thirds of the mozzarella cheese. Top with remaining pasta and sauce. Sprinkle with remaining mozzarella and Parmesan cheeses.

3. Cook, covered, over medium heat for 5 to 7 minutes or until heated through and cheeses, are melted. Let stand, covered, for 1 minute before serving.

PER SERVING *358 cal., 14 g fat (6 g sat. fat), 57 mg chol., 784 mg sodium, 32 g carb., 3 g fiber, 25 g pro.*

START TO FINISH 30 minutes

6 servings	ingredients	12 servings
3 cups	dried mafalda pasta (mini lasagna noodles)	6 cups
12 oz.	lean ground beef or bulk pork sausage	24 oz.
one 26-oz. jar	tomato-base pasta sauce	two 26-oz. jars
1½ cups	shredded part-skim mozzarella cheese	3 cups
¼ cup	grated Parmesan cheese	½ cup

Firehouse Chili

Turn to this easy-to-make chili to feed a crowd. It's extra-hearty served over macaroni.

1. In a 6- to 8-quart Dutch oven cook beef, onion, celery, and garlic until meat is browned and onion is tender; drain off fat. Stir in undrained chili beans, tomato sauce, undrained tomatoes, chili powder, and hot pepper sauce. Bring to boiling; reduce heat. Simmer, covered, for 2 hours.

2. Serve chili over hot cooked macaroni. If desired, top with sour cream, cheddar cheese and/or green onions, and pass hot pepper sauce.

PER SERVING *433 cal., 15 g fat (6 g sat. fat), 68 mg chol., 1,251 mg sodium, 48 g carb., 7 g fiber, 28 g pro.*

PREP 20 minutes
COOK 2 hours

5 servings	ingredients	10 servings
1 lb.	lean ground beef	2 lb.
½ large	onion, chopped	1 large
1½ stalks	celery, chopped	3 stalks
¾ tsp.	bottled minced garlic	1½ tsp.
half 30-oz. can	chili beans	one 30-oz. can
half 29-oz. can	tomato sauce	one 29-oz. can
half 28-oz. can	stewed tomatoes, cut up	one 28-oz. can
1 Tbsp.	chili powder	2 Tbsp.
1½ tsp.	bottled hot pepper sauce	1 Tbsp.
	Hot cooked macaroni	
	Sour cream and shredded cheddar cheese (optional)	
	Sliced green onions (optional)	
	Bottled hot pepper sauce (optional)	

Beef, Onion, and Sun-Dried Tomato Sandwiches

START TO FINISH 30 minutes

6 servings	ingredients	12 servings
1 to 1½ lb.	boneless beef sirloin steak or top round steak, cut 1 inch thick	2 to 3 lb.
½ tsp.	coarse ground black pepper	1 tsp.
1 Tbsp.	vegetable oil	2 Tbsp.
half large	red onion, sliced	1 large
6	ciabatta rolls	12
4 Tbsp.	mayonnaise	8 Tbsp.
2 cups	arugula, fresh basil, or spinach	4 cups
half 11.25-oz. jar	sun-dried tomato halves in oil	one 12.5-oz. jar

Allow the steak to rest at least 5 minutes before slicing it to allow juices to redistribute, rather than letting juices run on a cutting board.

1. Trim fat from meat. Evenly sprinkle pepper over both sides of meat; press in with your fingers. In a large heavy skillet cook meat in hot oil over medium heat for 15 to 20 minutes for medium rare (145°F) to medium (160°F), turning once. Remove meat, reserving drippings in skillet. Keep meat warm.

2. Add onion to reserved drippings. (Add more oil, if necessary.) Cook 5 to 10 minutes or until onion is nearly tender, stirring occasionally.

3. Meanwhile, split ciabatta rolls and, if desired, toast the rolls. When cool, spread with mayonnaise. Thinly slice meat across the grain into bite-size strips.

4. Layer rolls with arugula, meat, sun-dried tomato halves, and onion.

PER SERVING *335 cal., 8 g fat (3 g sat. fat), 46 mg chol., 227 mg sodium, 41 g carb., 4 g fiber, 26 g pro.*

Italian-Style French Dips

Make these sandwiches when you have leftover cooked beef or pork. Serve with a simple side of chips or green salad to have a satisfying dinner on the table in half an hour.

1. In a large saucepan melt butter over medium heat. Add sweet pepper and onion; cook and stir for 10 minutes or until tender. Stir in beef, broth, Italian seasoning, and black pepper. Bring to boiling; reduce heat. Simmer, uncovered, for 5 minutes.

2. Using a slotted spoon, divide meat and vegetables among French rolls. If desired, top with cheese. Skim fat from cooking liquid. Serve sandwiches with bowls of cooking liquid for dipping.

PER SERVING *367 cal., 16 g fat (7 g sat. fat), 88 mg chol., 700 mg sodium, 24 g carb., 2 g fiber, 30 g pro.*

START TO FINISH **30 minutes**

4 servings	ingredients	8 servings
2 Tbsp.	butter or vegetable oil	¼ cup
1 cup	thin strips green sweet pepper	2 cups
1 medium	onion, cut into thin wedges	2 medium
2 cups	shredded cooked beef or pork	4 cups
one 14.5-oz. can	beef broth	two 14.5-oz. cans
1½ tsp.	dried Italian seasoning, crushed	3 tsp.
¼ tsp.	black pepper	½ tsp.
4	French rolls, split and toasted	8
	Shredded Swiss, provolone, or Monterey Jack cheese (optional)	

Flank Steak Vinaigrette Salad

PREP 30 minutes
GRILL 15 minutes

4 servings	ingredients	8 servings
⅓ cup	cider vinegar	⅔ cup
3 Tbsp.	olive oil	6 Tbsp.
2 Tbsp.	snipped fresh cilantro	¼ cup
1 to 2 tsp.	sugar	2 to 4 tsp.
1½ tsp.	red wine vinegar	3 tsp.
1 tsp.	coarse ground mustard	2 tsp.
¼ tsp.	salt	½ tsp.
⅛ tsp.	black pepper	¼ tsp.
¾ cup	finely chopped green sweet pepper	1½ cups
¼ cup	peeled and finely chopped jicama	½ cup
2 Tbsp.	finely chopped red onion	¼ cup
½	fresh serrano chile pepper, seeded and chopped (tip, page 11)	1
8 oz.	beef flank steak	16 oz.
12 oz.	tiny new potatoes, quartered	24 oz.
8 oz.	fresh sugar snap pea pods, trimmed (if desired)	16 oz.
6 cups	mixed salad greens	12 cups

Fresh sweet pepper, snap peas, and jicama add pleasant crunch to this steak salad. Slice the meat across the grain to ensure each bite is perfectly tender.

1. For cilantro-pepper vinaigrette, in a medium bowl whisk together cider vinegar, oil, cilantro, sugar, red wine vinegar, mustard, salt, and black pepper. Stir in sweet pepper, jicama, onion, and serrano pepper. Cover and chill until needed.

2. Trim fat from steak. Grill steak, covered, over medium heat for 15 to 17 minutes for medium (160°F), turning once. Thinly slice meat; transfer to a bowl; cover and chill until needed.

3. Meanwhile, in a large covered saucepan cook potatoes in enough lightly salted boiling water to cover for 10 minutes. Add pea pods. Cook 1 minute more; drain. Rinse with cold water; drain again.

4. Pour half the vinaigrette over steak; toss gently to coat. Pour remaining vinaigrette over potatoes and pea pods; toss gently. Place greens on a serving platter; top with potatoes, pea pods, and steak.

PER SERVING *210 cal., 15 g fat (3 g sat. fat), 26 mg chol., 225 mg sodium, 27 g carb., 5 g fiber, 17 g pro.*

Flank Steak with Antipasto

Scoring flank steak before marinating it allows the seasonings to penetrate deeply into the meat.

1. Trim fat from steak. Score both sides in a diamond pattern by making shallow diagonal cuts at 1-inch intervals. Place in a resealable plastic bag set in a shallow dish. For marinade, pour ½ cup of the Italian dressing over steak. Seal bag; turn to coat steak. Marinate in the refrigerator for 20 minutes or up to 24 hours.

2. Meanwhile, for antipasto topping, in a medium bowl combine tomatoes, artichoke hearts, mozzarella pearls, and basil. Drizzle with remaining Italian dressing; toss gently to coat.

3. Drain steak, discarding marinade. Grill steak, covered, over medium heat for 13 to 17 minutes for medium rare (145°F) or 17 to 21 minutes for medium (160°F), turning once. Cover and let stand 5 minutes. Serve steak with antipasto topping.

PER SERVING *274 cal., 11 g fat (5 g sat. fat), 98 mg chol., 529 mg sodium, 8 g carb., 2 g fiber, 35 g pro.*

START TO FINISH **45 minutes**

4 servings	ingredients	8 servings
1¼ lb.	beef flank steak	2½ lb.
¾ cup	bottled fat-free or regular Italian salad dressing	1½ cup
1 cup	grape or cherry tomatoes, quartered	2 cups
¾ cup	canned artichoke hearts, sliced	1½ cups
½ cup	fresh mozzarella cheese pearls or chopped fresh mozzarella cheese	1 cup
½ cup	thinly sliced fresh basil	1 cup

Honey-Balsamic Beef Stir-Fry

PREP 25 minutes
COOK 10 minutes

4 servings	ingredients	8 servings
12 oz.	beef sirloin steak or beef top round steak	24 oz.
¾ cup	beef broth	1½ cups
3 Tbsp.	reduced-sodium soy sauce	6 Tbsp.
2 Tbsp.	balsamic vinegar	¼ cup
2 Tbsp.	honey	¼ cup
2 Tbsp.	cornstarch	¼ cup
¼ tsp.	crushed red pepper	½ tsp.
2 Tbsp.	vegetable oil	¼ cup
1 Tbsp.	finely chopped, peeled fresh ginger	2 Tbsp.
2 medium	red sweet peppers, seeded and cut into bite-size strips	4 medium
1 medium	red onion, cut into thin wedges	2 medium
4 cups	thin strips bok choy or baby bok choy	8 cups
2 cups	hot cooked rice or linguine	4 cups

Freeze the steak about 30 minutes before cutting it into thin strips. Partially frozen meat is easier to slice thinly and evenly.

1. Trim fat from steak; thinly slice across the grain into bite-size strips.

2. For sauce, in a small bowl whisk together broth, soy sauce, vinegar, honey, cornstarch, and crushed red pepper; set aside.

3. In an extra-large skillet heat half the oil over medium-high heat. Add ginger; cook and stir for 15 seconds. Add sweet peppers and onion; cook and stir for 5 minutes. Add bok choy; cook and stir for 2 to 3 minutes more or until vegetables are crisp-tender. Remove vegetables from skillet.

4. Add remaining oil to skillet; add beef to skillet. Cook and stir 2 to 3 minutes. Push beef to edge of skillet. Stir sauce until well combined. Add sauce to center of skillet. Cook and stir until thickened and bubbly. Return cooked vegetables to skillet. Stir all ingredients together to coat with sauce. Cook and stir 1 minute more. Spoon stir-fry over rice.

PER SERVING *424 cal., 15 g fat (4 g sat. fat), 42 mg chol., 713 mg sodium, 51 g carb., 3 g fiber, 21 g pro.*

Sesame Ginger Beef Stir-Fry

When you need dinner fast, turn to this recipe. Once the meat is sliced, the sauce mixed, and the vegetables chopped, this stir-fry can be on the table in less than 10 minutes.

1. If desired, partially freeze beef for easy slicing. Trim fat from meat. Thinly slice meat across the grain into bite-size strips. For sauce, in a small bowl stir together broth, ginger, cornstarch, garlic, coriander, and crushed red pepper. Set aside.

2. In a wok or large skillet heat oil over medium-high heat. Add onion; cook and stir in hot oil 2 minutes. Add broccoli and sweet pepper. Cook and stir 1 to 2 minutes or until vegetables are crisp-tender. Remove from wok.

3. Add beef strips to hot wok. Cook and stir 2 to 3 minutes or until meat is slightly pink in center. Push meat from center of wok.

4. Stir sauce; add to center of wok. Cook and stir until thickened and bubbly. Return cooked vegetables to wok; stir to coat all ingredients with sauce. Cook and stir 1 to 2 minutes more or until heated through. Serve with rice. Sprinkle with sesame seeds, if desired.

*TIP If desired, for 4 servings use 1 teaspoon ground ginger for the fresh ginger. For 8 servings, use 2 teaspoons ground ginger for the fresh ginger.

PER SERVING *255 cal., 7 g fat (2 g sat. fat), 36 mg chol., 212 mg sodium, 25 g carb., 4 g fiber, 23 g pro.*

START TO FINISH **30 minutes**

4 servings	ingredients	8 servings
12 oz.	beef sirloin	24 oz.
1 cup	reduced-sodium chicken broth	2 cups
1 Tbsp.	grated fresh ginger*	2 Tbsp.
1 Tbsp.	cornstarch	2 Tbsp.
2 cloves	garlic, minced	4 cloves
1 tsp.	ground coriander	2 tsp.
⅛ to ¼ tsp.	crushed red pepper	¼ to ½ tsp.
2 tsp.	sesame oil	4 tsp.
1 medium	onion, halved and sliced	2 medium
2 cups	broccoli florets	4 cups
1 medium	red sweet pepper, cut in bite-size strips	2 medium
1⅓ cups	hot cooked brown rice	2⅔ cups
1 tsp.	sesame seeds, toasted (tip, page 12) (optional)	2 tsp.

Pasta with Garlicky Steak and Red Onions

Parmigiano-Reggiano cheese gives this Italian-style skillet dinner big flavor at serving time. To make shavings, run a vegetable peeler along the surface of the cheese.

1. Cook pasta in lightly salted water according to package directions. Drain, reserving ¼ cup of the pasta cooking water. Return pasta to hot pan; cover and keep warm.

2. Meanwhile, trim fat from meat. Thinly slice meat across the grain into bite-size strips. In an extra-large nonstick skillet heat half the oil over medium-high heat. Add meat; cook and stir 3 to 4 minutes or until meat is slightly pink in center. Remove from skillet; keep warm.

3. Add red onion, garlic, salt, and crushed red pepper to skillet. Cook 8 minutes or until onion is tender, stirring occasionally. Add broth and the reserved pasta cooking water; bring to boiling.

4. Add remaining oil, the beef, onion mixture, spinach, and basil to cooked pasta; toss just until spinach is wilted. If desired, sprinkle servings with cheese.

PER SERVING *358 cal., 9 g fat (1 g sat. fat), 39 mg chol., 476 mg sodium, 45 g carb., 6 g fiber, 25 g pro.*

START TO FINISH **30 minutes**

6 servings	ingredients	12 servings
12 oz.	dried regular or multigrain penne pasta	24 oz.
12 oz.	boneless beef sirloin steak	24 oz.
2 Tbsp.	olive oil	¼ cup
1	medium red onion, quartered and thinly sliced	2
4 cloves	garlic, minced	8 cloves
¾ tsp.	salt	1½ tsp.
¼ tsp.	crushed red pepper	½ tsp.
1 cup	reduced-sodium chicken broth	2 cups
4 cups	fresh baby spinach	8 cups
1 Tbsp.	snipped fresh basil or thyme	2 Tbsp.
¼ cup	shaved Parmigiano-Reggiano cheese or Parmesan cheese (optional)	½ cup

Gingered Beef and Broccoli Salad Bowl

This super fast recipe borrows a familiar flavor combination from beef stir-fry—ginger, broccoli, and sweet pepper—and transforms it into a fresh, bright green salad.

1. Trim fat from steak. Thinly slice steak across the grain into bite-size strips; set aside.

2. In a large skillet heat 2 tablespoons of the vinaigrette over medium-high heat. Add broccoli. Cook and stir for 3 minutes. Add beef to skillet. Cook and stir 2 to 3 minutes or until beef is slightly pink in center. Stir in sweet pepper.

3. Divide greens among bowls. Top with beef stir-fry. Drizzle with remaining salad dressing.

FOR 8 SERVINGS In Step 2 use 4 tablespoons of the vinaigrette.

PER SERVING *237 cal., 9 g fat (2 g sat. fat), 60 mg chol., 468 mg sodium, 17 g carb., 4 g fiber, 22 g pro.*

START TO FINISH **20 minutes**

4 servings	ingredients	8 servings
12 oz.	beef sirloin steak	24 oz.
⅔ cup	bottled ginger vinaigrette	1⅓ cups
3 cups	broccoli florets	6 cups
8 cups	mixed spring or baby salad greens	16 cups
1	red sweet pepper, seeded and cut into strips	2
	Sesame seeds, toasted (tip, page 12)	

Pork Chops with Spinach-Apricot Stuffing

A food processor speeds up prep for this recipe. Use it to make soft bread crumbs and to finely chop onion and celery.

1. For stuffing, in a medium saucepan heat half the oil over medium heat. Add onion and celery; cook until tender, stirring occasionally. Stir in spinach, bread crumbs, and dried apricots; cook 1 minute or until spinach is wilted. Remove from heat.

2. Trim fat from chops. Make a pocket in each chop by cutting horizontally from the fat side almost to bone on the opposite side. Spoon stuffing into pockets. If necessary, secure openings with wooden toothpicks. Sprinkle chops with herbes de Provence, salt, and pepper.

3. In a large skillet heat remaining oil over medium-high heat. Add chops; reduce heat to medium. Cook 10 to 13 minutes or until a thermometer registers 145°F, turning once. Let chops stand 3 minutes before serving.

PER SERVING *407 cal., 19 g fat (5 g sat. fat), 128 mg chol., 469 mg sodium, 9 g carb., 1 g fiber, 48 g pro.*

START TO FINISH **40 minutes**

4 servings	ingredients	8 servings
2 Tbsp.	olive oil	4 Tbsp.
½ cup	finely chopped onion	1 cup
½ cup	finely chopped celery	1 cup
2 cups	coarsely chopped fresh spinach leaves	4 cups
½ cup	soft bread crumbs	1 cup
¼ cup	snipped dried apricots	½ cup
4 (3 lb. total)	bone-in pork loin chops, cut 1¼ inches thick	8 (6 lb. total)
1 tsp.	dried herbes de Provence, crushed	2 tsp.
½ tsp.	salt	1 tsp.
⅛ tsp.	black pepper	¼ tsp.

Pancetta-Stuffed Pork Chops alla Fiorentina

Bone-in chops retain moistness and flavor while cooking. Choose chops that have vibrant pink color with no gray spots and a moist—not wet—surface.

1. Trim fat from chops. Make a pocket in each chop by cutting horizontally from the fat side almost to bone. Place chops in a resealable plastic bag set in an extra-large bowl. For marinade, in a small bowl combine oil, lemon peel, 2 tablespoons rosemary, 4 cloves garlic, salt, and pepper. Pour marinade over chops. Seal bag; turn to coat chops. Marinate in the refrigerator 4 to 24 hours, turning bag occasionally.

2. For stuffing, in a large skillet cook and stir onion and pancetta over medium-high heat for 6 to 8 minutes or until pancetta is browned and crisp. Remove from heat. Stir in bread crumbs, 2 teaspoons rosemary, snipped oregano, and 2 cloves garlic. Stir in lemon juice.

3. Drain chops, discarding marinade. Spoon stuffing into pockets in chops; press tops of chops lightly to secure stuffing.

4. Prepare grill for indirect heat, using a drip pan. Place chops over drip pan. Grill, covered, over indirect medium heat for 25 to 30 minutes or until chops are slightly pink in center and juices run clear (145°F). Let chops stand 3 minutes before serving. If desired, top with oregano leaves.

FOR 8 SERVINGS In Step 1 use the ¼ cup rosemary and 8 cloves garlic. In Step 2 use the 4 teaspoons rosemary and 4 cloves garlic.

PER SERVING *621 cal., 47 g fat (10 g sat. fat), 127 mg chol., 677 mg sodium, 10 g carb., 2 g fiber, 39 g pro.*

PREP **25 minutes**
MARINATE **4 hours**
GRILL **25 minutes**
STAND **5 minutes**

4 servings	ingredients	8 servings
4	bone-in pork loin chops or rib chops, cut 1¼ inches thick	8
½ cup	olive oil	1 cup
3 Tbsp.	finely shredded lemon peel	6 Tbsp.
2 Tbsp.	finely snipped fresh rosemary	¼ cup
4 cloves	garlic, minced	8 cloves
½ tsp.	salt	1 tsp.
½ tsp.	freshly ground black pepper	1 tsp.
1 cup	chopped onion	2 cups
2 oz.	pancetta, finely chopped	4 oz.
½ cup	soft bread crumbs	1 cup
2 tsp.	finely snipped fresh rosemary	4 tsp.
1 tsp.	snipped fresh oregano	2 tsp.
2 cloves	garlic, minced	4 cloves
1 Tbsp.	lemon juice	2 Tbsp.
	Small fresh oregano leaves (optional)	

Fruit-Filled Pork Tenderloin

These special sandwiches boast a stuffing of dried fruit and warm spices. No dinner rolls on hand for serving? Opt instead for a simple salad or vegetable alongside the pork.

1. Preheat oven to 425°F. For stuffing, in a small saucepan bring port just to boiling. Remove from heat. Stir in raisins, dried cranberries, dried apricots, and apple pie spice. Cover and let stand for 15 minutes. Transfer to a food processor and process for 10 to 15 seconds or until coarsely ground.

2. Make a lengthwise cut along the center of tenderloin, cutting almost to but not through the opposite side. Spread open. Place tenderloin between two pieces of plastic wrap. Using the flat side of a meat mallet, pound lightly from center to edges to slightly less than ½ inch thick. Remove plastic wrap.

3. Divide fruit filling between meat portions, spreading to within ½ inch of edges. Starting from a long side, roll each portion into a spiral. Tie at 2-inch intervals with 100% cotton kitchen string. Sprinkle rolls with salt and pepper.

4. Place tenderloin on a rack in a shallow roasting pan. Roast 20 to 30 minutes or until thermometer registers 145°F. Remove from oven. Cover loosely with foil; let stand 10 minutes before slicing.

5. Remove and discard string. Slice tenderloin. If desired, serve in dinner rolls with mustard.

PER SERVING *241 cal., 2 g fat (1 g sat. fat), 64 mg chol., 199 mg sodium, 30 g carb., 2 g fiber, 22 g pro.*

PREP **35 minutes**
STAND **25 minutes**
ROAST **25 minutes**

4 servings	ingredients	8 servings
¼ cup	ruby port wine or pomegranate juice	½ cup
6 Tbsp.	golden raisins	¾ cup
6 Tbsp.	dried cranberries	¾ cup
⅓ cup	dried apricots, quartered	⅔ cup
⅛ tsp.	apple pie spice	¼ tsp.
one 14- to 18-oz.	pork tenderloins	two 14- to 18-oz.
¼ tsp.	salt	½ tsp.
⅛ tsp.	black pepper	¼ tsp.
	Dinner rolls (optional)	
	Coarse-grain, Dijon, or honey mustard (optional)	

Grilled Pork and Pear Stir-Fry

Threading pork pieces onto skewers makes easy work for grilling. Allow space—about ¼ inch—between each piece to ensure the pork cooks evenly.

1. Trim fat from pork; cut into 1-inch pieces. Thread pork onto wooden* or metal skewers, allowing ¼ inch between pieces. For sauce, in a small bowl stir together preserves, soy sauce, and crushed red pepper; set aside.

2. In a grill wok or tray combine pears, sweet pepper, snow peas, water chestnuts, oil, and ginger.

3. Grill pork kabobs and pear mixture, covered, over medium heat for 12 to 15 minutes or until pork is slightly pink in center, turning once. Brush pork with some of the sauce during the last minute of grilling. Stir pear mixture two or three times during grilling.

4. Remove pork from skewers. Transfer pork and pear mixture to a large bowl. Add the remaining sauce; toss gently to coat. Serve stir-fry over hot cooked rice. If desired, sprinkle with almonds.

***TIP** If using wooden skewers soak them in water at least 30 minutes before threading the pork.

PER SERVING *401 cal., 8 g fat (2 g sat. fat), 74 mg chol., 327 mg sodium, 55 g carb., 5 g fiber, 27 g pro.*

PREP 25 minutes
GRILL 12 minutes

4 servings	ingredients	8 servings
1 lb.	pork tenderloin	2 lb.
¼ cup	plum preserves or jam	½ cup
1 Tbsp.	soy sauce	2 Tbsp.
⅛ to ¼ tsp.	crushed red pepper	¼ to ½ tsp.
2 cups	sliced firm ripe pears	4 cups
1 cup	yellow or red sweet pepper strips	2 cups
1 cup	fresh snow peas, halved crosswise	2 cups
half 8-oz. can	sliced water chestnuts, drained	one 8-oz. can
1 Tbsp.	vegetable oil	2 Tbsp.
2 tsp.	grated fresh ginger	4 tsp.
2 cups	hot cooked rice	4 cups
2 Tbsp.	sliced almonds, toasted (tip, page 12) (optional)	¼ cup

Thai Pork Stir-Fry

Thai-style seasoning adds to the quick preparation of this recipe. Just one ingredient adds lemongrass, lime zest, ginger, mint, chile, and other flavor-packed spices to the stir-fry.

1. In a small bowl whisk together coconut milk, flour, and Thai seasoning; set aside. Trim fat from pork, if necessary, and cut into thin strips; set aside.

2. Meanwhile, in a large nonstick skillet heat one-third of the olive oil over medium-high heat. Add thawed vegetables to hot skillet. Cover and cook 3 to 5 minutes or just until vegetables are crisp-tender, stirring occasionally. Remove vegetables from skillet.

3. Add remaining oil to skillet. Add pork strips. Cook and stir over medium-high heat for 3 to 5 minutes or just until cooked through. Return vegetables to skillet; stir coconut milk mixture then add to skillet. Cook and stir 1 to 2 minutes or until sauce is thickened and bubbly. Serve over hot cooked rice.

PER SERVING *281 cal., 8 g fat (3 g sat. fat), 74 mg chol., 321 mg sodium, 23 g carb., 2 g fiber, 26 g pro.*

START TO FINISH **20 minutes**

4 servings	ingredients	8 servings
½ cup	reduced-fat unsweetened coconut milk	1 cup
1 Tbsp.	all-purpose flour	2 Tbsp.
1 Tbsp.	Thai-style seasoning blend	2 Tbsp.
1 lb.	boneless pork loin	2 lb.
3 tsp.	olive oil	6 tsp.
one 14.4-oz. pkg.	frozen sweet pepper stir-fry vegetables, thawed and well drained	two 14.4-oz. pkg.
1⅓ cups	hot cooked brown rice	2⅔ cups

Miso Soup with Pork and Edamame

Look for miso paste—fermented soybean paste, which is popular in Japanese cooking—in the Asian section of the supermarket or at Asian food stores.

1. Trim fat from meat. Cut meat into 1-inch pieces. In a 4-quart Dutch oven heat half the oil over medium-high heat. Add meat; cook until browned, stirring occasionally. Remove meat and set aside.

2. In the same Dutch oven heat the remaining oil over medium heat. Add sweet pepper and onion; cook 5 minutes, stirring occasionally. Add ginger, garlic, and black pepper; cook and stir 30 seconds more. Add 7 cups of the water; bring to boiling.

3. Meanwhile, in a small bowl gradually whisk remaining water into the miso paste. Stir miso paste, meat, and edamame into mixture in Dutch oven. Return to boiling; reduce heat. Simmer, covered, for 3 minutes. Stir in cabbage. Simmer, uncovered, 2 minutes more, stirring occasionally. Sprinkle with radishes to serve.

FOR 12 SERVINGS In Step 2 add 14 cups water.

PER SERVING *216 cal., 9 g fat (1 g sat. fat), 39 mg chol., 486 mg sodium, 14 g carb., 5 g fiber, 20 g pro.*

START TO FINISH **30 minutes**

6 servings	ingredients	12 servings
12 oz.	boneless pork loin roast	24 oz.
4 tsp.	canola oil	3 Tbsp.
¾ cup	chopped red sweet pepper	1½ cups
½ cup	chopped onion	1 cup
1 Tbsp.	grated fresh ginger	2 Tbsp.
2 cloves	garlic, minced	4 cloves
⅛ tsp.	black pepper	¼ tsp.
8 cups	water	16 cups
¼ cup	red miso paste	½ cup
one 10- to 12-oz. pkg.	frozen shelled sweet soybeans (edamame)	two 10- to 12-oz. pkg.
4 cups	thinly sliced savoy cabbage	8 cups
2 to 3	radishes, thinly sliced	4 to 6

Caramelized Pork with Cantaloupe Salsa

Make this recipe when the freshest, most flavorful cantaloupe are available—in late summer. Look for cantaloupe that are firm and heavy for their size and have a sweet, fruity fragrance.

1. Remove rind and seeds from cantaloupe; chop cantaloupe. In a food processor or blender process 2 cups of the chopped cantaloupe and the orange juice until smooth. Set remaining chopped cantaloupe aside.

2. For sauce, transfer ½ cup of the pureed cantaloupe to a small bowl; stir in hoisin sauce. Set aside. Press remaining cantaloupe puree through a fine-mesh sieve placed over a bowl. Discard solids. Set juice aside.

3. Lightly sprinkle chops with salt and pepper; brush generously with some of the sauce. In an extra-large skillet heat oil over medium-high heat. Add chops to skillet; cook 6 to 8 minutes or until browned and slightly pink inside (145°F), turning once. Remove chops from skillet; let stand 3 minutes.

4. Meanwhile, for the salsa, in a large bowl combine chopped cantaloupe and juice, and green onions.

5. Add the remaining sauce to the skillet; cook and stir until heated through. Serve chops with sauce, salsa and, if desired, cabbage.

FOR 8 SERVINGS In Step 1 use 4 cups of the chopped cantaloupe. In Step 2 transfer 1 cup of the pureed cantaloupe to a small bowl.

PER SERVING *327 cal., 10 g fat (2 g sat. fat), 117 mg chol., 452 mg sodium, 19 g carb., 2 g fiber, 39 g pro.*

START TO FINISH **25 minutes**

4 servings	ingredients	8 servings
1	small cantaloupe	2
¼ cup	orange juice	½ cup
3 Tbsp.	hoisin sauce	6 Tbsp.
4	pork loin rib chops, cut ½ inch thick	8
	Salt	
	Black pepper	
1 Tbsp.	vegetable oil	2 Tbsp.
3	green onions, thinly sliced	6
	Shredded napa cabbage (optional)	

Pork-Wasabi Tacos

Fresh napa cabbage, carrots, and cucumber add cool crunch to this Asian spin on pork tacos. To shred the cabbage, cut the head into quarters, remove the core, then thinly slice it.

1. Thread pork on wooden or metal skewers*. Brush with hoisin sauce. Grill pork, covered, over medium heat for 11 to 13 minutes (145°F), turning once. Add flatbreads the last 1 minute of grilling, turning once.

2. Meanwhile, for wasabi oil, in a small bowl whisk together wasabi paste, the water, oil, vinegar, and sugar. If desired, stir in green onions.

3. Serve pork with cabbage, carrots, and cucumber in warm flatbreads; drizzle with wasabi oil.

***TIP** If using wooden skewers soak them in water at least 30 minutes before threading pork.

PER SERVING *447 cal., 13 g fat (5 g sat. fat), 89 mg chol., 470 mg sodium, 50 g carb., 2 g fiber, 31 g pro.*

PREP **25 minutes**
GRILL **11 minutes**

6 servings	ingredients	12 servings
one 1½-lb.	pork tenderloin, cut into 1-inch pieces	two 1½-lb.
⅓ cup	hoisin sauce	⅔ cup
6	flatbreads or flour tortillas	12
1 to 2 tsp.	prepared wasabi paste	2 to 4 tsp.
2 Tbsp.	water	¼ cup
2 Tbsp.	vegetable oil	¼ cup
½ tsp.	white wine vinegar	1 tsp.
½ tsp.	sugar	1 tsp.
2	green onions, thinly sliced (optional)	4
¼ head	napa cabbage, shredded	½ head
2	carrots, shredded	4
½	English cucumber, thinly sliced	1

Pork and Noodle Salad

This main-dish salad comes together in just 20 minutes then is chilled from 2 to 24 hours. When fresh asparagus isn't available, swap in broccoli florets or green beans.

PREP 20 minutes
CHILL 2 hours

4 servings	ingredients	8 servings
4 oz.	dried Chinese egg noodles or fine noodles, broken in half	8 oz.
¼ cup	reduced-sodium soy sauce	½ cup
2 Tbsp.	rice vinegar or cider vinegar	¼ cup
1 Tbsp.	canola or vegetable oil	2 Tbsp.
1 Tbsp.	honey	2 Tbsp.
1 tsp.	sesame oil	2 tsp.
¾ lb.	fresh asparagus, trimmed and cut into 2-inch pieces	1½ lb.
2	carrots, cut into thin strips	4
8 oz.	cooked lean pork, cut into thin strips	16 oz.
	Sliced green onions (optional)	
	Sesame seeds (optional)	

1. Cook pasta according to package directions; drain.

2. Meanwhile, for vinaigrette, in a screw-top jar combine soy sauce, rice vinegar, canola oil, honey, and sesame oil. Cover and shake well. Chill 2 to 24 hours.

3. Cook asparagus in a covered saucepan in a small amount of lightly salted boiling water for 4 to 6 minutes or until crisp-tender.

4. In a large bowl combine noodles, asparagus, carrots, and pork. Cover and chill 2 to 24 hours.

5. Pour vinaigrette over salad; toss gently to coat. If desired, sprinkle with green onions and sesame seeds.

PER SERVING *328 cal., 12 g fat (3 g sat. fat), 76 mg chol., 974 mg sodium, 31 g carb., 2 g fiber, 24 g pro.*

Quick Pork Fried Brown Rice

Five-spice powder is used extensively in Chinese cooking and it's the key to the aromatic flavor of this stir-fry. The pungent spice mix includes cinnamon, cloves, fennel, star anise, and szechuan pepper.

1. In a large nonstick skillet heat 1 tablespoon of the oil over medium-high heat. Add eggs; cook, stirring gently, until set. Remove cooked eggs; cool slightly then cut into strips.

2. In the same skillet heat remaining oil over medium-high heat. Add green onions, ginger, garlic, and five-spice powder; cook and stir about 45 seconds or until very fragrant.

3. Add brown rice, pork, and peas and carrots. Cook 2 minutes or until heated through, stirring frequently. Drizzle with soy sauce. Gently stir in egg strips; cook 1 minute more.

FOR 8 SERVINGS In Step 1 use 2 tablespoons of the oil.

PER SERVING *351 cal., 13 g fat (2 g sat. fat), 119 mg chol., 368 mg sodium, 40 g carb., 4 g fiber, 19 g pro.*

START TO FINISH **20 minutes**

4 servings	ingredients	8 servings
3 Tbsp.	canola oil	6 Tbsp.
2	eggs, lightly beaten	4
1 bunch	green onions, thinly sliced	2 bunches
1 Tbsp.	grated fresh ginger	2 Tbsp.
2 cloves	garlic, minced	4 cloves
½ tsp.	Chinese five-spice powder	1 tsp.
two 10-oz. pkg.	frozen cooked brown rice, prepared according to package directions	four 10-oz. pkg.
1 cup	cubed cooked pork tenderloin, chicken breast, or ham	2 cups
1 cup	frozen peas and carrots, thawed	2 cups
2 Tbsp.	reduced-sodium soy sauce	¼ cup

CHAPTER 4

Seafood

Bring something new to the table with these creative fish and seafood recipes. Each boasts fast cooking times and promises scrumptious results.

111

118

130

Cajun-Rubbed Salmon

Searing the salmon gives it a deliciously crisp crust. For optimal browning, pat dry all the excess moisture from the salmon before adding the Cajun seasoning.

START TO FINISH 30 minutes

4 servings	ingredients	8 servings
four 6-oz.	fresh or frozen boneless salmon fillets	eight 6-oz.
½ cup	slivered red onion	1 cup
½ cup	chopped celery	1 cup
2 Tbsp.	snipped fresh Italian parsley	¼ cup
2 Tbsp.	chopped dill pickle	¼ cup
1 Tbsp.	dill pickle juice	2 Tbsp.
3 Tbsp.	olive oil	6 Tbsp.
2 tsp.	Dijon mustard	4 tsp.
¼ tsp.	salt	½ tsp.
Dash	sugar	⅛ tsp.
2 Tbsp.	Cajun seasoning	¼ cup

1. Thaw salmon, if frozen. Preheat oven to 400°F. For relish, in a small bowl combine onion, celery, parsley, pickle, pickle juice, 1 tablespoon of the oil, the mustard, salt, and sugar. Cover and chill until ready to serve (up to 1 hour).

2. Rinse salmon; pat dry with paper towels. Measure thickness of salmon. Sprinkle salmon with Cajun seasoning; rub in with your fingers.

3. In a large cast-iron or heavy oven-going skillet heat remaining oil over medium-high heat. Add salmon, skin side up; cook 2 to 3 minutes or until lightly browned. Turn salmon. Place skillet in oven. Roast until salmon begins to flake when tested with a fork. (Allow 4 to 6 minutes total per ½-inch thickness of salmon, including browning time.) Serve salmon with relish.

FOR 8 SERVINGS In Step 1 use 2 tablespoons olive oil.

PER SERVING *356 cal., 21 g fat (3 g sat. fat), 94 mg chol., 778 mg sodium, 5 g carb., 1 g fiber, 34 g pro.*

Chile-Glazed Salmon Burgers

An Asian-style slaw—seasoned with a savory mix of soy sauce and toasted sesame oil—provides crunch to these spicy salmon burgers.

1. Thaw salmon, if frozen. Rinse salmon; pat dry with paper towels. Cut into 1-inch pieces. Place salmon, half at a time, in a food processor. Cover and process until finely chopped. In a large bowl combine egg, green onions, salt, and black pepper. Add chopped salmon; mix gently until combined. Using damp hands, shape mixture into six ½-inch-thick patties. Cover and chill at least 30 minutes.

2. Meanwhile, in a small bowl combine mayonnaise and Asian chili sauce. Cover and chill until needed.

3. For slaw, in a large bowl whisk together vegetable oil, vinegar, soy sauce, sugar, and sesame oil. Add shredded cabbage and cilantro; toss to coat.

4. Lightly brush both sides of salmon patties with additional vegetable oil.

5. Grill patties, covered, for 6 to 8 minutes or until done (160°F), turning and brushing once with Asian chile sauce. Grill buns, cut sides down, for 1 to 2 minutes or until lightly toasted.

6. Spread cut sides of buns with mayonnaise-chile sauce. Serve patties on buns with slaw and cucumber slices.

PER SERVING *589 cal., 35 g fat (5 g sat. fat), 123 mg chol., 942 mg sodium, 28 g carb., 2 g fiber, 36 g pro.*

PREP 30 minutes
CHILL 30 minutes
GRILL 6 minutes

6 servings	ingredients	12 servings
2 lb.	fresh or frozen skinless, boneless salmon fillets	4 lb.
1	egg, lightly beaten	2
¼ cup	thinly sliced green onions	½ cup
½ tsp.	salt	1 tsp.
½ tsp.	black pepper	1 tsp.
⅔ cup	mayonnaise	1⅓ cups
2 Tbsp.	Asian chile sauce (sriracha sauce)	¼ cup
1 Tbsp.	vegetable oil or canola oil	2 Tbsp.
1 Tbsp.	rice vinegar	2 Tbsp.
1 Tbsp.	soy sauce	2 Tbsp.
1 tsp.	sugar	2 tsp.
1 tsp.	toasted sesame oil	2 tsp.
4 cups	shredded cabbage with carrot (coleslaw mix)	8 cups
¼ cup	snipped fresh cilantro	½ cup
	Vegetable oil or canola oil	
	Asian sweet chile sauce	
6	sesame seed hamburger buns, split	12
1 cup	thinly sliced seedless cucumber	2 cups

Salmon and Wilted Greens

This quick-to-the-table salmon recipe calls for only four additional ingredients—one of them a flavorful sesame-ginger salad dressing.

1. Thaw salmon, if frozen. Preheat broiler. Grease the rack of an unheated broiler pan. Rinse fish; pat dry with paper towels. If necessary, cut fish into four serving-size pieces. Place fish on prepared rack of broiler pan. Broil 4 inches from heat for 6 to 9 minutes or until fish flakes easily when tested with a fork, brushing with the 1 tablespoon dressing halfway through broiling time. Cover; keep warm.

2. Meanwhile, in a salad bowl combine spinach and orange sections. In a large skillet bring the ½ cup dressing to boiling. Boil gently, uncovered, for 1 minute. Remove from heat. Pour over spinach salad; toss to coat. Divide salad among serving plates. Top with salmon.

FOR 8 SERVINGS In Step 1 use the 2 tablespoons salad dressing. In Step 2 use the 1 cup salad dressing

PER SERVING *397 cal., 25 g fat (5 g sat. fat), 67 mg chol., 623 mg sodium, 20 g carb., 3 g fiber, 24 g pro.*

START TO FINISH **20 minutes**

4 servings	ingredients	8 servings
1 lb.	fresh or frozen salmon fillets	2 lb.
1 Tbsp.	bottled sesame-ginger salad dressing	2 Tbsp.
6 cups	fresh baby spinach or torn mixed salad greens	12 cups
1 medium	orange, peeled and sectioned	2 medium
½ cup	bottled sesame-ginger salad dressing	1 cup

Salmon Satay with Cucumber-Feta Salad

A Greek-inspired cucumber salad accompanies these citrusy salmon kabobs. If you can't find a seedless cucumber—such as an English or hothouse variety—use a seeded and peeled regular cucumber instead.

1. Thaw salmon, if frozen. Rinse salmon; pat dry with paper towels. Cut salmon into twelve ½-inch-wide strips. In a medium bowl stir together salmon strips and salad dressing. Cover with plastic wrap; marinate in refrigerator for 45 minutes (do not marinate any longer). Thinly slice two of the lemons, six slices each (12 slices total). Juice remaining lemon for 3 tablespoons juice; set slices and juice aside.

2. For cucumber salad, in a large bowl combine cucumber, feta, onion, and olives. Add the lemon juice, oil, mint, parsley, snipped dill, salt, and pepper; stir gently to combine. Cover and chill until ready to serve.

3. Remove salmon strips from marinade, reserving marinade. Thread two strips, accordion-style, onto each 12-inch skewer*, alternating salmon with folded lemon slices.

4. Grill kabobs, covered, over medium heat for 6 to 9 minutes or until fish flakes easily when tested with a fork, turning and brushing once with reserved marinade. Discard remaining marinade. Serve kabobs with cucumber salad. If desired, sprinkle with fresh dill sprigs.

FOR 12 SERVINGS In Step 1 slice four lemons (6 slices each; 24 slices total). Juice remaining lemons for 6 tablespoons lemon juice.

*TIP If using wooden skewers, soak in water 30 minutes before threading salmon strips.

PER SERVING *490 cal., 36 g fat (11 g sat. fat), 96 mg chol., 844 mg sodium, 16 g carb., 3 g fiber, 30 g pro.*

PREP **30 minutes**
MARINATE **45 minutes**
GRILL **6 minutes**

6 servings	ingredients	12 servings
1½ lb.	fresh or frozen skinless salmon fillet	3 lb.
½ cup	bottled white balsamic vinaigrette dressing	1 cup
3	lemons	6
1 large	seedless cucumber, diced	2 large
8 oz.	feta cheese, cut into ¼-inch cubes	16 oz.
½ cup	chopped red onion	1 cup
⅓ cup	coarsely chopped pitted Kalamata olives	⅔ cup
¼ cup	olive oil	½ cup
1 Tbsp.	snipped fresh mint	2 Tbsp.
1 Tbsp.	snipped fresh Italian parsley	2 Tbsp.
1 Tbsp.	snipped fresh dill	2 Tbsp.
½ tsp.	salt	1 tsp.
¼ tsp.	freshly ground black pepper	½ tsp.
	Fresh dill sprigs (optional)	

Smoked Salmon Flatbread

Make these simple and satisfying pitas for a super speedy dinner. No cooking required—just set out the ingredients for each diner to assemble the pitas at the table.

1. Spread cream cheese on one side of the flatbread. Top with the lettuce. Add salmon, radishes, and capers; sprinkle with pepper. Fold in half to serve.

PER SERVING *284 cal., 16 g fat (9 g sat. fat), 45 mg chol., 824 mg sodium, 21 g carb., 9 g fiber, 18 g pro.*

START TO FINISH **20 minutes**

6 servings	ingredients	12 servings
one 8-oz. tub	cream cheese spread with chive and onion	two 8-oz. tubs
6	multigrain flatbread or Greek pita flatbread	12
3 cups	torn lettuce	6 cups
8 oz.	hot smoked salmon, broken into pieces	16 oz.
8	small radishes, thinly sliced	16
2 Tbsp.	capers, rinsed and drained	¼ cup
	Black pepper	

Planked Sesame-Ginger Tuna Steaks

Wooden grilling planks impart savory, aromatic flavor to fish. Soaking the plank in water before grilling is important—it increases flavor-boosting smoke production and keeps the wood from going up in flames while the fish cooks. Look for grilling planks at specialty food or cookware stores.

1. Thaw tuna, if frozen. At least 1 hour before grilling, soak plank in enough water to cover, weighting the plank to submerge during soaking.

2. For sauce, in a small bowl combine plum sauce, soy sauce, ginger, vinegar, oil, and crushed red pepper.

3. Heat plank on a greased grill rack, uncovered, over medium heat for 3 to 5 minutes or until plank begins to crackle and smoke. Turn plank over. Meanwhile, grill tuna for 2 to 3 minutes or until grill marks appear. Place tuna steaks, grilled sides up, on plank. Grill, covered, for 10 to 15 minutes or until tuna begins to flake easily when tested with a fork and is still pink in the center. Add pineapple to grill the last 8 to 10 minutes of grilling or until grill marks appear, turning once.

4. Transfer tuna and pineapple to a serving platter. Drizzle tuna steaks with sauce; sprinkle with sesame seeds. If desired, sprinkle with green onions.

*TIP If desired, substitute swordfish or halibut steaks for the tuna steaks.

PER SERVING *292 cal., 2 g fat (1 g sat. fat), 66 mg chol., 434 mg sodium, 24 g carb., 2 g fiber, 43 g pro.*

SOAK 1 hour
PREP 25 minutes
GRILL 12 minutes

4 servings	ingredients	8 servings
4	fresh or frozen tuna steaks, 1 to 1½ inches thick*	8
1	alder or cedar grilling plank	2
¼ cup	bottled plum sauce	½ cup
1 Tbsp.	soy sauce	2 Tbsp.
2 tsp.	grated fresh ginger	4 tsp.
1 tsp.	rice vinegar	2 tsp.
½ tsp.	toasted sesame oil	1 tsp.
¼ tsp.	crushed red pepper	½ tsp.
1 medium	fresh pineapple, peeled, cored, and cut into 8 spears	2 medium
1 tsp.	sesame seeds and/or black sesame seeds, toasted (tip, page 12)	2 tsp.
	Chopped green onions (optional)	

Fast Niçoise Salad

This French-style salad calls for the traditional combination of tuna, hard-boiled eggs, potatoes, and tiny niçoise olives. If you can't find niçoise olives, use Kalamata olives or ripe black olives.

4 servings	ingredients	8 servings
1 Tbsp.	butter	2 Tbsp.
2 cups	refrigerated red-skin potato wedges	4 cups
6 cups	packaged mixed salad greens	12 cups
three 3-oz. pouches	solid white (albacore) tuna (water pack)	six 3-oz. pouches
1 cup	cherry tomatoes	2 cups
4	hard-cooked eggs, quartered*	8
	Pitted niçoise olives (optional)	
⅓ cup	bottled roasted garlic vinaigrette salad dressing	⅔ cup
	Salt and freshly ground black pepper	

1. In a large skillet melt butter over medium heat. Add potatoes; cook, covered, about 15 minutes or until golden, stirring occasionally.

2. Meanwhile, divide salad greens among plates. Top with tuna, tomatoes, hard-cooked eggs, and, if desired, olives. Divide potatoes among plates. Drizzle with salad dressing; sprinkle with salt and pepper.

*TIP To hard-cook eggs, place them in a single layer in a saucepan. Add enough cold water to cover eggs by 1 inch. Bring to a rapid boil over high heat (water will have large rapidly breaking bubbles). Remove from heat, cover, and let stand 15 minutes; drain. Place eggs in ice water for 15 minutes or until cool enough to handle; drain. To peel, gently tap each egg on countertop. Roll the egg between the palms of your hands. Peel off eggshell, starting at the large end. Use immediately or refrigerate in an airtight container.

PER SERVING *308 cal., 15 g fat (5 g sat. fat), 220 mg chol., 1,112 mg sodium, 16 g carb., 4 g fiber, 25 g pro.*

Quick Fish Stew with Basil Gremolata

Gremolata—a popular topping for stews and braises served in Italy—is a flavorful mix of citrus zest, fresh herbs, and garlic. It gives this seafood stew a bright, flavorful finish.

1. Thaw cod and shrimp, if frozen. Rinse cod and shrimp; pat dry with paper towels. Cut cod into 1-inch pieces. Set cod and shrimp aside.

2. In a large saucepan or Dutch oven heat oil over medium heat. Add sweet pepper, onion, and half the garlic; cook until tender, stirring occasionally. Stir in tomatoes, the water, salt, and black pepper. Bring to boiling. Stir in cod and shrimp. Return to boiling; reduce heat. Simmer, covered, for 2 to 3 minutes or until cod begins to flake when tested with a fork and shrimp are opaque.

3. For basil gremolata, in a small bowl combine basil, lemon peel, and remaining garlic. Ladle stew into bowls. Sprinkle with basil gremolata.

PER SERVING *197 cal., 5 g fat (1 g sat. fat), 83 mg chol., 686 mg sodium, 19 g carb., 5 g fiber, 19 g pro.*

START TO FINISH **25 minutes**

4 servings	ingredients	8 servings
6 oz.	fresh or frozen cod fillets	12 oz.
6 oz.	fresh or frozen peeled and deveined shrimp	12 oz.
1 Tbsp.	olive oil	2 Tbsp.
1 cup	green sweet pepper strips	2 cups
1 cup	chopped onion	2 cups
4 cloves	garlic, minced	8 cloves
two 14.5-oz. cans	Italian-style stewed tomatoes, undrained and cut up	four 14.5-oz. cans
½ cup	water	1 cup
¼ tsp.	salt	½ tsp.
¼ tsp.	black pepper	½ tsp.
3 Tbsp.	snipped fresh basil	6 Tbsp.
1 Tbsp.	finely shredded lemon peel	2 Tbsp.

Tilapia Vera Cruz

Just about any mild-flavor white fish will work well for this recipe, so choose your family's favorite. Serve the dish with rice or bread to soak up flavorful cooking juices.

1. Thaw fish, if frozen. Rinse fish; pat dry with paper towels. Set aside.

2. In an extra-large skillet heat oil over medium heat. Add onion, jalapeño, if using, and garlic; cook 2 to 3 minutes or until onion is tender, stirring occasionally. Stir in tomatoes, mushrooms, olives, oregano, salt, and black pepper. Bring to boiling.

3. Carefully add fish to skillet, spooning tomato mixture over fish. Return to boiling; reduce heat. Simmer, covered, for 8 to 10 minutes or until fish begins to flake when tested with a fork. If desired, break fish into chunks. Serve with rice and/or bread.

*TIP If desired, for 4 servings, substitute ½ teaspoon dried oregano, crushed, for the fresh oregano, For 8 servings, substitute 1 teaspoon dried oregano, crushed, for the fresh oregano.

PER SERVING *363 cal., 10 g fat (2 g sat. fat), 84 mg chol., 1,111 mg sodium, 31 g carb., 3 g fiber, 38 g pro.*

START TO FINISH **25 minutes**

4 servings	ingredients	8 servings
four 6- to 8-oz.	fresh or frozen skinless tilapia, red snapper, mahi mahi, or other fish fillets	eight 6- to 8-oz.
1 Tbsp.	olive oil	2 Tbsp.
1	small onion, cut into thin wedges	2
1	fresh jalapeño, seeded and finely chopped (tip, page 11) (optional)	2
1 clove	garlic, minced	2 cloves
one 14.5-oz. can	diced tomatoes, undrained	two 14.5-oz. cans
1 cup	sliced fresh cremini or button mushrooms	2 cups
¾ cup	pimiento-stuffed green olives, coarsely chopped	1½ cups
1 Tbsp.	snipped fresh oregano*	2 Tbsp.
¼ tsp.	salt	½ tsp.
⅛ tsp.	black pepper	¼ tsp.
2 cups	hot cooked rice and/or 8 crusty bread slices	4 cups

Fish Tostadas with Chili-Lime Cream

Broiling the fish instead of frying it keeps these open-face fish tacos light and healthful. Fish has delicate texture and is easily overcooked. To prevent that, check it at the minimum cooking time. To test for doneness, insert a fork into the fish and gently twist. When it flakes, it's done.

1. Thaw fish, if frozen. Rinse fish; pat dry with paper towels. Sprinkle fish with half the chili powder and the salt; set aside. Preheat broiler. Grease the rack of an unheated broiler pan; set aside.

2. For chili-lime cream, into a small bowl squeeze half a lime for 2 teaspoons juice. Stir in sour cream, garlic powder, and remaining chili powder; set aside. Cut remaining lime half into wedges; set aside.

3. Place fish on prepared rack of broiler pan; tuck under thin edges to make fish an even thickness. Measure thickness of fish. Place tostada shells on a baking sheet; place in oven on the lowest rack. Broil fish 4 inches from heat for 4 to 6 minutes per ½-inch thickness or until fish flakes easily when tested with a fork. Remove fish and tostada shells from oven. Break fish into chunks. Top tostada shells with fish, chili-lime cream, coleslaw mix, avocado (if desired), tomatoes, and hot pepper sauce (if desired). Serve with lime wedges.

FOR 8 SERVINGS In Step 2 squeeze one whole lime for 4 teaspoons lime juice and cut the remaining whole lime into wedges.

PER SERVING *278 cal., 14 g fat (5 g sat. fat), 67 mg chol., 303 mg sodium, 17 g carb., 2 g fiber, 25 g pro.*

PREP 15 minutes
BROIL 4 minutes per ½-inch thickness

4 servings	ingredients	8 servings
1 lb.	fresh or frozen tilapia or cod fillets	2 lb.
½ tsp.	chili powder	1 tsp.
¼ tsp.	salt	½ tsp.
1	lime, halved	2
½ cup	sour cream	1 cup
½ tsp.	garlic powder	1 tsp.
eight 6-inch	tostada shells	sixteen 6-inch
2 cups	packaged shredded cabbage with carrot (coleslaw mix)	4 cups
1	avocado, halved, seeded, peeled, and sliced (optional)	2
1 cup	cherry tomatoes, quartered	2 cups
	Bottled hot pepper sauce (optional)	

Mediterranean Cod with Roasted Tomatoes

The serve-along for this fish, Israeli couscous, has larger granules than regular couscous. If you can't find it, substitute regular couscous or orzo, cooked according to package directions.

1. Preheat oven to 450°F. Thaw fish, if frozen. Rinse fish; pat dry with paper towels. In a small bowl combine snipped oregano, snipped thyme, salt, garlic powder, paprika, and black pepper. Sprinkle half of the herb mixture on all sides of fish fillets.

2. Line a 15×10×1-inch baking pan with foil; coat foil with cooking spray. Place fish on one side of the pan; place tomatoes and garlic on opposite side. Combine remaining herb mixture with the oil. Drizzle over tomatoes and garlic; toss to coat. Bake 8 to 12 minutes or until fish flakes easily when tested with a fork, stirring tomatoes once. Stir olives and capers into tomatoes.

3. Meanwhile, in a saucepan combine the water and couscous. Bring to boiling; reduce heat. Simmer, covered, 12 to 15 minutes or until tender.

4. Sprinkle fish, couscous, and roasted tomatoes with fresh oregano and/or thyme leaves.

FOR 8 SERVINGS In Step 2 use two baking pans.

PER SERVING *243 cal., 5 g fat (1 g sat. fat), 49 mg chol., 428 mg sodium, 25 g carb., 3 g fiber, 24 g pro.*

PREP 30 minutes
BAKE 8 minutes
COOK 12 minutes

4 servings	ingredients	8 servings
four 4-oz.	fresh or frozen skinless cod fillets, ¾- to 1-inch thick	eight 4-oz.
2 tsp.	snipped fresh oregano	4 tsp.
1 tsp.	snipped fresh thyme	2 tsp.
½ tsp.	salt	1 tsp.
¼ tsp.	garlic powder	½ tsp.
¼ tsp.	paprika	½ tsp.
¼ tsp.	black pepper	½ tsp.
	Nonstick cooking spray	
1 Tbsp.	olive oil	2 Tbsp.
3 cups	cherry tomatoes	6 cups
2 cloves	garlic, sliced	4 cloves
2 Tbsp.	sliced pitted ripe olives	¼ cup
2 tsp.	capers	4 tsp.
1 cup	water	2 cups
⅔ cup	Israeli couscous (large pearl)	1⅓ cups
	Fresh oregano and/or thyme leaves	

Smoky Cod with Sweet Potatoes

Chipotle peppers—which are smoked jalapeño peppers—impart spicy, smoky flavor to this skillet-braised fish. Look for them canned in adobo sauce with Mexican foods.

1. Thaw fish, if frozen. Rinse fish and pat dry; set aside. In a small bowl combine clam juice, white wine, and cornstarch; set aside. For chipotle aïoli, in another bowl combine mayonnaise, chipotle pepper, vinegar, and mustard. Cover and chill.

2. Sprinkle cod pieces with ¼ teaspoon of the salt and the pepper. Lightly coat with flour, shaking off excess. Heat an extra-large stainless-steel skillet over medium-high heat until a bead of water vaporizes within 2 seconds of contact. Swirl in 2 tablespoons of peanut oil. Add cod pieces; cook undisturbed, 2 minutes, or until opaque and browned on the bottom. Using a metal spatula, turn fillets over; cook 2 to 3 minutes more or until opaque and browned. Transfer to a plate. Use spatula to break cod into chunks; set aside.

3. Heat remaining peanut oil pan over medium-high heat. Add sweet potato and onion; cook 4 minutes, scraping up browned bits. Add corn and remaining salt; cook and stir 1 minute. Add clam juice mixture; bring to boiling. Boil gently, uncovered, for 2 minutes. Return cod to pan. Cover; reduce heat to medium. Cook 1 to 2 minutes or just until cod is cooked through and potatoes are tender. Top with chipotle aïoli. Sprinkle with parsley.

* If using frozen corn, thaw and pat dry before using.

FOR 8 SERVINGS In Step 2 use ½ teaspoon of the salt and 4 tablespoons of the peanut oil.

PER SERVING *461 cal., 27 g fat (4 g sat. fat), 56 mg chol., 1,082 mg sodium, 28 g carb., 3 g fiber, 28 g pro.*

START TO FINISH **35 minutes**

4 servings	ingredients	8 servings
1 lb.	½- to ¾-inch thick fresh or frozen cod filets	2 lb.
1 cup	clam juice	2 cups
½ cup	dry white wine	1 cup
1 tsp.	cornstarch	2 tsp.
⅓ cup	mayonnaise	⅔ cup
1	canned chipotle chile pepper in adobo sauce, chopped	2
2 tsp.	white wine vinegar	4 tsp.
1 tsp.	Dijon mustard	2 tsp.
¾ tsp.	salt	1½ tsp.
¼ tsp.	freshly ground black pepper	½ tsp.
2 Tbsp.	all-purpose flour	¼ cup
3 Tbsp.	peanut oil or vegetable oil	6 Tbsp.
1 medium (2 cups)	sweet potato, peeled, halved lengthwise, and very thinly sliced	2 medium (4 cups)
1 large	onion, cut in thin wedges	2 large
1½ cups	fresh or frozen sweet corn kernels*	3 cups
¼ cup	finely snipped fresh Italian parsley	½ cup

Seared Scallops with Noodle Salad

When buying sea scallops, choose ones that have uniform pearly white color and fresh ocean scent. They should be firm enough to retain their shape when touched.

1. Thaw scallops, if frozen. Cook fettuccine according to package directions; drain. Rinse with cold water; drain again. In a large bowl combine orange juice, vinegar, sesame oil, lime peel, ginger, and half the salt. Add cooked fettuccine, spinach, cucumber, and daikon; toss gently to coat. Set aside.

2. Rinse scallops; pat dry with paper towels. Sprinkle with remaining salt and the pepper.

3. Coat a large nonstick skillet with cooking spray; heat skillet over medium-high heat. Add scallops. Cook 3 to 5 minutes or until scallops are opaque, turning once. Serve scallops with fettuccine. Sprinkle with sesame seeds.

PER SERVING *297 cal., 10 g fat (2 g sat. fat), 31 mg chol., 817 mg sodium, 31 g carb., 2 g fiber, 19 g pro.*

START TO FINISH **30 minutes**

4 servings	ingredients	8 servings
12 (18 oz.)	fresh or frozen sea scallops	24 (36 oz.)
4 oz.	dried brown rice fettuccine or banh pho (Vietnamese wide rice noodles)	8 oz.
¼ cup	orange juice	½ cup
2 Tbsp.	rice vinegar	¼ cup
2 Tbsp.	toasted sesame oil	¼ cup
1 tsp.	finely shredded lime peel	2 tsp.
1 tsp.	grated fresh ginger	2 tsp.
½ tsp.	salt	1 tsp.
1½ cups	chopped fresh spinach leaves	3 cups
1 cup	chopped cucumber	2 cups
⅔ cup	coarsely shredded daikon or thinly sliced radishes	1⅓ cups
¼ tsp.	ground black pepper	½ tsp.
	Nonstick cooking spray	
2 Tbsp.	sesame seeds, toasted (tip, page 12)	¼ cup

Thai Coconut and Basmati Rice with Seared Scallops

Basmati rice is an aromatic rice popular in India and Middle-Eastern countries. It has a nutty fragrance and taste that complements rich coconut milk and sweet mango.

1. Thaw scallops, if frozen. Rinse scallops; pat dry with paper towels. Sprinkle scallops with half the salt.

2. In a medium saucepan heat the 2 teaspoons oil. Add onion and cook over medium heat 5 to 7 minutes or until tender. Stir in rice. Cook and stir 1 minute more. Stir in coconut milk, broth, the water, remaining salt, and the pepper. Bring to boiling; reduce heat. Simmer, covered, about 20 minutes or until rice is tender and liquid is absorbed. Stir in mango and snipped basil.

3. Meanwhile, in a large nonstick skillet heat the 1 tablespoon oil. Add scallops and cook over medium-high heat 2 to 3 minutes or until opaque and golden brown, turning once halfway through cooking time. Serve scallops over rice. If desired, sprinkle with basil leaves.

FOR 8 SERVINGS In Step 2 use the 4 teaspoons oil. In Step 3 use the 2 tablespoons oil.

PER SERVING *299 cal., 9 g fat (3 g sat. fat), 37 mg chol., 518 mg sodium, 32 g carb., 1 g fiber, 22 g pro.*

PREP **20 minutes**
COOK **30 minutes**

4 servings	ingredients	8 servings
1 lb.	fresh or frozen sea scallops	2 lb.
½ tsp.	salt	1 tsp.
2 tsp.	olive oil	4 tsp.
½ cup	chopped onion	1 cup
½ cup	uncooked basmati rice	1 cup
¾ cup	unsweetened light coconut milk	1½ cups
¼ cup	reduced-sodium chicken broth	½ cup
¼ cup	water	½ cup
¼ tsp.	black pepper	½ tsp.
1	medium mango, seeded, peeled, and coarsely chopped	2
¼ cup	snipped fresh basil	½ cup
1 Tbsp.	olive oil	2 Tbsp.
	Fresh basil leaves (optional)	

Shrimp, Scallop, and Veggie Stir-Fry

When sea scallops are not available, buy small bay scallops, which can be left whole for this fast and fresh recipe.

1. Cut scallops in half horizontally. Set aside.

2. In a small bowl combine orange juice, soy sauce, cornstarch, ground ginger, and crushed red pepper.

3. Coat an extra-large nonstick skillet or wok with nonstick spray and heat over high heat until hot. Stir-fry the broccoli and sweet pepper 2 minutes or until the broccoli is bright green. Add fresh ginger and garlic; stir-fry for 15 seconds, until fragrant. Add mushrooms, reserved scallops, shrimp, and orange juice mixture. Cook 3 to 4 minutes, stirring, until scallops and shrimp are opaque and cooked through. Serve immediately over hot cooked rice.

PER SERVING *215 cal., 2 g fat (0 g sat. fat), 67 mg chol., 598 mg sodium, 32 g carb., 5 g fiber, 18 g pro.*

START TO FINISH **30 minutes**

4 servings	ingredients	8 servings
8 oz.	scallops	16 oz.
½ cup	orange juice	1 cup
1 Tbsp.	reduced-sodium soy sauce	2 Tbsp.
2 tsp.	cornstarch	4 tsp.
½ tsp.	ground ginger	1 tsp.
⅛ tsp.	crushed red pepper	¼ tsp.
	Nonstick cooking spray	
4 cups	small broccoli florets	8 cups
1 large	red sweet pepper, seeded cut into strips	2 large
2 tsp.	finely shredded fresh ginger	4 tsp.
1 clove	garlic, minced	2 cloves
1 cup	shiitake mushrooms, stemmed and sliced	2 cups
6 oz.	medium shrimp, peeled and deveined	12 oz.
1⅓ cups	hot cooked brown rice	2⅔ cups

Shrimp and Watermelon Salad

For this summer salad, look for shrimp that are firm and translucent with fresh, ocean-like scent. Avoid shrimp with black spots or any trace of off odor, which indicates they are past their prime.

1. Thaw shrimp, if frozen. Rinse shrimp; pat dry with paper towels. In a large skillet heat half the oil over medium-high heat. Add shrimp; cook and stir 3 to 4 minutes or until shrimp are opaque. Transfer shrimp to a bowl; stir in snipped thyme.

2. Add remaining oil, the bok choy, and tomatoes to hot skillet; cook and stir 1 minute. Return shrimp to skillet; cook 1 minute more. Season to taste with salt and pepper.

3. Arrange shrimp, vegetables, and watermelon on plates. Squeeze lime juice over all; sprinkle with thyme sprigs and, if desired, feta cheese.

PER SERVING *241 cal., 9 g fat (1 g sat. fat), 172 mg chol., 363 mg sodium, 16 g carb., 2 g fiber, 25 g pro.*

START TO FINISH **20 minutes**

4 servings	ingredients	8 servings
1 lb.	fresh or frozen peeled, deveined medium shrimp	2 lb.
2 Tbsp.	olive oil	¼ cup
2 tsp.	snipped fresh thyme	4 tsp.
4 cups	sliced bok choy or napa cabbage	8 cups
1 cup	grape tomatoes, halved	2 cups
	Salt	
	Black pepper	
two 1-inch slices	seedless watermelon, halved	four 1-inch slices
	Small limes, halved	
	Fresh thyme sprigs	
	Feta cheese (optional)	

Coconut Shrimp with Mango Rice Pilaf

These oven-fried coconut shrimp are easier to prepare and lower in fat than the traditionally fried version. The speedy brown rice pilaf—studded with sweet mango and fresh cilantro—fills out this tropical-inspired meal.

START TO FINISH 30 minutes

4 servings	ingredients	8 servings
1 lb.	fresh or frozen extra-large shrimp in shells	2 lb.
	Nonstick cooking spray	
2	egg whites, lightly beaten	4
¾ cup	finely crushed reduced-fat or reduced-sodium shredded wheat crackers	1½ cups
⅓ cup	shredded coconut	⅔ cup
¼ tsp.	ground ginger	½ tsp.
¼ tsp.	black pepper	½ tsp.
one 8.8-oz. pouch	cooked brown rice	two 8.8-oz. pouches
½ cup	chopped fresh or refrigerated mango	1 cup
⅓ cup	sliced green onions	⅔ cup
2 Tbsp.	snipped fresh cilantro	¼ cup

1. Thaw shrimp, if frozen. Preheat oven to 450°F. Lightly coat a large baking sheet with cooking spray; set aside. Peel and devein shrimp, leaving tails intact if desired. Rinse shrimp; pat dry with paper towels.

2. Pour egg whites into a shallow dish. In another shallow dish combine crushed crackers, coconut, ginger, and pepper. Dip shrimp into egg, turning to coat. Dip into coconut mixture, pressing to coat (leave tail uncoated).

3. Arrange shrimp on prepared baking sheet. Bake 8 to 10 minutes or until shrimp are opaque and coating is lightly browned.

4. Meanwhile, for pilaf, heat rice according to package directions. Transfer to a serving bowl. Stir in mango and green onions. Serve shrimp with pilaf and sprinkle with cilantro.

PER SERVING *303 cal., 7 g fat (2 g sat. fat), 129 mg chol., 249 mg sodium, 36 g carb., 3 g fiber, 23 g pro.*

CHAPTER 5

Sides

Find tasty complements to main dishes with this collection of extraordinary breads, salads, vegetables, and soups.

137

145

156

Fresh Cranberry Scones

For a sweet-savory dinner, serve these easy-to-make scones alongside roasted pork or poultry. When fresh cranberries are unavailable, you can use thawed frozen cranberries instead.

1. Preheat oven to 375°F. In a bowl stir together flour, granulated sugar, baking powder, and salt. Make a well in the center of flour mixture; set aside.

2. In another bowl stir together the cranberries and honey; stir in whipping cream. Add cranberry mixture to flour mixture all at once. Using a fork, stir just until moistened.

3. Turn dough out onto a lightly floured surface. Fold and gently press dough 10 to 12 strokes or until dough is nearly smooth. (Dough may appear pink.) Pat or lightly roll dough into an 8-inch square. Cut into nine squares. Place squares about 1 inch apart on an ungreased baking sheet. In a bowl stir together the egg and the water. Lightly brush squares with egg mixture and sprinkle with coarse sugar.

4. Bake 20 to 25 minutes or until tops are golden brown. Remove scones from baking sheet; serve warm.

PER SERVING *300 cal., 12 g fat (7 g sat. fat), 68 mg chol., 184 mg sodium, 42 g carb., 2 g fiber, 6 g pro.*

PREP **20 minutes**
BAKE **20 minutes**

9 servings	ingredients	18 servings
2¼ cups	all-purpose flour	4½ cups
2 Tbsp.	granulated sugar	¼ cup
1 Tbsp.	baking powder	2 Tbsp.
¼ tsp.	salt	½ tsp.
1½ cups	fresh cranberries, finely chopped	3 cups
2 Tbsp.	honey	¼ cup
1 cup	whipping cream	2 cups
1	egg, lightly beaten	2
1 Tbsp.	water	2 Tbsp.
	Coarse sugar	

Grilled Bread and Veggie Kabobs

Cutting zucchini into ribbons speeds cooking time as it cooks alongside the bread and other veggies.

PREP 25 minutes
GRILL 3 minutes

4 servings	ingredients	8 servings
2 to 3 cups	1-inch cubes sourdough or Italian bread	4 to 6 cups
2 Tbsp.	olive oil	¼ cup
2 tsp.	lemon juice	4 tsp.
1 tsp.	garlic salt	2 tsp.
½ to 1 tsp.	dried herb-pepper seasoning	1 to 2 tsp.
1 medium	zucchini	2 medium
8 oz. (about 12)	whole fresh mushrooms, halved	1 lb. (about 24)
2 cups	red and/or yellow cherry tomatoes	4 cups

1. Place bread cubes in a large bowl. In a small bowl combine oil, lemon juice, garlic salt, and herb-pepper seasoning. Drizzle half the oil mixture over bread cubes; toss gently to coat.

2. Using a vegetable peeler, cut zucchini lengthwise into long, thin ribbons, cutting to seeds. Repeat on opposite side. (Discard or save center piece of zucchini for another use.) In another large bowl combine zucchini ribbons, mushrooms, and cherry tomatoes. Drizzle with the remaining oil mixture; toss gently to coat.

3. On eight 10-inch metal skewers alternately thread vegetables and bread cubes, threading zucchini accordion style and leaving ¼ inch between all of the pieces.

4. Grill kabobs, covered, over medium heat for 3 to 5 minutes or until vegetables are tender and bread just starts to brown, turning once.

PER SERVING *169 cal., 8 g fat (1 g sat. fat), 0 mg chol., 379 mg sodium, 22 g carb., 3 g fiber, 6 g pro.*

SERVING SUGGESTIONS Arrange kabobs on mixed salad greens and drizzle with vinaigrette. Or serve with Mediterranean Eggplant Dip (recipe, page 20) or Roasted Red Pepper-Chipotle Hummus (recipe, page 21).

Skillet-Roasted Vegetables

This stovetop saute of bright-color vegetables is simply seasoned with freshly squeezed lemon juice and cilantro.

1. Trim and peel beets, reserving ½ cup of the green tops. Cut beets into ½-inch wedges.

2. Peel the sweet potato, then cut into quarters lengthwise. Cut quarters into 2-inch pieces.

3. In an extra-large skillet heat oil over medium heat. Add beets, sweet potato, and quartered new potatoes; cook, covered, for 10 minutes, turning occasionally. Cook, uncovered, 10 to 15 minutes or until vegetables are tender and browned on all sides, turning occasionally. Add pea pods; sprinkle with salt and pepper. Cook, covered, 2 to 3 minutes more or until pea pods are crisp-tender. Stir in reserved beet greens.

4. Sprinkle vegetables with cilantro and lemon juice; toss gently to coat. Serve with lemon wedges.

FOR 12 SERVINGS In Step 1 reserve 1 cup of the green tops.

PER SERVING *116 cal., 5 g fat (1 g sat. fat), 0 mg chol., 146 mg sodium, 17 g carb., 3 g fiber, 2 g pro.*

PREP **20 minutes**
COOK **22 minutes**

6 servings	ingredients	12 servings
8 oz.	assorted small beets	16 oz.
1 small	sweet potato	2 small
8 oz.	tiny new potatoes and/or small fingerling potatoes, quartered	16 oz.
2 to 3 Tbsp.	peanut oil	4 to 6 Tbsp.
1 cup	sugar snap pea pods or snow pea pods, trimmed if desired	2 cups
¼ tsp.	salt	½ tsp.
⅛ tsp.	freshly ground black pepper	¼ tsp.
¼ cup	snipped fresh cilantro or Italian parsley	½ cup
2 Tbsp.	lemon juice	¼ cup
	Lemon wedges	

Skillet Corn

This updated version of succotash calls for edamame beans—rather than traditional lima beans—plus fresh tomatoes and jalapeño chile pepper. It's topped with tangy lime-garlic dressing and crisp-cooked bacon.

1. In a large skillet cook bacon over medium heat until crisp. Remove bacon and drain on paper towels, reserving 2 tablespoons drippings in skillet. Crumble bacon; set aside. Add corn and soybeans to reserved drippings. Cook and stir 3 to 4 minutes or just until vegetables are crisp-tender.

2. In bowl combine corn mixture, tomatoes, red onion, cilantro, and jalapeño.

3. For dressing, in a small screw-top jar combine oil, lime peel, lime juice, garlic, cumin, salt, and chili powder. Cover and shake well. Pour dressing over salad; toss gently to coat. Sprinkle with crumbled bacon.

FOR 12 SERVINGS In Step 1 reserve about 4 tablespoons drippings in skillet.

PER SERVING *182 cal., 11 g fat (3 g sat. fat), 9 mg chol., 160 mg sodium, 17 g carb., 3 g fiber, 7 g pro.*

START TO FINISH **35 minutes**

6 servings	ingredients	12 servings
4 slices	bacon	8 slices
2 cups	fresh or frozen whole kernel corn	4 cups
1 cup	frozen shelled sweet soybeans (edamame)	2 cups
1 cup	grape tomatoes or cherry tomatoes, halved	2 cups
½ medium	red onion, thinly sliced	1 medium
2 Tbsp.	snipped fresh cilantro	¼ cup
1 small	fresh jalapeño, seeded and finely chopped (tip, page 11)	2 small
1 Tbsp.	olive oil	2 Tbsp.
½ tsp.	finely shredded lime peel	1 tsp.
1 Tbsp.	lime juice	2 Tbsp.
2 cloves	garlic, minced	4 cloves
¼ tsp.	ground cumin	½ tsp.
⅛ tsp.	salt	¼ tsp.
⅛ tsp.	chili powder	¼ tsp.

Asparagus with Mushroom Cream Sauce

For distinct mushroom flavor, use wild mushrooms—such as shiitake, oyster, or cremini—in the cream sauce for this spring or early-summer side dish.

1. Prepare a large bowl of ice water. Snap off and discard woody bases from asparagus. In a covered Dutch oven cook asparagus in a small amount of boiling water for 4 to 6 minutes or just until crisp-tender; drain. Immediately plunge asparagus into the ice water; cool. Remove asparagus; pat dry with paper towels. Set aside.

2. For sauce, in a large skillet heat oil over medium-high heat. Add onion, garlic, salt, and pepper; cook until onion is tender, stirring occasionally. Stir in broth, sherry, and cream cheese. Bring to boiling. Add mushrooms; cook 3 to 4 minutes or until mushrooms are tender and sauce is slightly thickened, stirring occasionally. Stir in Parmesan cheese. Serve asparagus with sauce and sprinkle with fresh thyme.

PER SERVING 242 cal., 10 g fat (2 g sat. fat), 7 mg chol., 429 mg sodium, 28 g carb., 11 g fiber, 15 g pro.

START TO FINISH **40 minutes**

4 servings	ingredients	8 servings
4 lb.	asparagus spears	8 lb.
2 Tbsp.	olive oil	¼ cup
1 cup	chopped onion	2 cups
6 cloves	garlic, minced	12 cloves
½ tsp.	salt	1 tsp.
½ tsp.	black pepper	1 tsp.
½ cup	reduced-sodium chicken broth or reduced-sodium vegetable broth	1 cup
¼ cup	dry sherry or dry white wine	½ cup
¼ cup	reduced-fat cream cheese (Neufchâtel)	½ cup
12 oz.	assorted sliced fresh mushrooms, such as button, shiitake, cremini, and/or oyster mushrooms	1½ lb.
1½ Tbsp.	grated Parmesan cheese	3 Tbsp.
2 tsp.	snipped fresh thyme	4 tsp.

Green Beans with Sage and Mushrooms

8 servings	ingredients	16 servings
2 lb.	fresh green beans, trimmed, if desired	4 lb.
2 Tbsp.	olive oil	¼ cup
2 Tbsp.	butter	¼ cup
3 to 4 cloves	garlic, thinly sliced	6 to 8 cloves
12 oz.	fresh mushrooms, such as cremini, button, porcini, or stemmed shiitake, halved lengthwise	1½ lb.
3 Tbsp.	snipped fresh sage	6 Tbsp.
	Coarse sea salt	
	Freshly ground black pepper	

If you use shiitake mushrooms, cut off the tough woody stems before slicing them.

1. In a large covered saucepan cook green beans in a small amount of salted boiling water for 3 to 4 minutes or just until crisp-tender; drain. Immediately plunge beans into ice water; let stand 3 minutes. Drain and set aside.

2. In an extra-large skillet heat oil and butter over medium heat. Add garlic; cook and stir just until golden brown. Add mushrooms; cook 6 to 8 minutes or until tender, stirring occasionally. Add green beans. Cook 5 to 8 minutes or until heated through, stirring occasionally. Remove from heat. Stir in sage. Season to taste with salt and pepper.

PER SERVING *112 cal., 6 g fat (2 g sat. fat), 8 mg chol., 150 mg sodium, 14 g carb., 4 g fiber, 3 g pro.*

Brussels Sprouts Salad with Hazelnuts

Rather than thinly slicing the Brussels sprouts yourself, save time by purchasing packaged shaved Brussels spouts. Look for them near salad mixes.

1. Trim stems and remove any wilted outer leaves from Brussels sprouts. Thinly slice sprouts.* In a microwave-safe dish combine Brussels sprouts and the water; cover with vented plastic wrap. Cook on high for 3 minutes or until sprouts are bright green, stirring once. Drain in a colander. Rinse with cold water to cool; drain again. Pat dry with paper towels or use a salad spinner to dry.

2. In a large bowl combine Brussels sprouts, hazelnuts, and the shredded cheese. For dressing, in a small screw-top jar combine vinegar, oil, salt, and pepper. Cover and shake well to combine. Pour dressing over salad; toss gently to coat. If desired, top with shaved cheese.

***TIP** To thinly slice Brussels sprouts, use the thin slicing blade of a food processor. Or halve the sprouts lengthwise with a sharp knife, then place halves, cut sides down, on the cutting board and thinly slice. Or use packaged shaved Brussels sprouts, available in many grocery stores.

PER SERVING *141 cal., 12 g fat (2 g sat. fat), 5 mg chol., 146 mg sodium, 6 g carb., 3 g fiber, 5 g pro.*

START TO FINISH **25 minutes**

8 servings	ingredients	16 servings
1 lb.	Brussels sprouts	2 lb.
2 Tbsp.	water	¼ cup
½ cup	hazelnuts (filberts), toasted and coarsely chopped (tip, page 54)	1 cup
½ cup (2 oz.)	finely shredded Pecorino Romano cheese	1 cup (4 oz.)
¼ cup	red wine vinegar	½ cup
3 Tbsp.	olive oil	6 Tbsp.
¼ tsp.	salt	½ tsp.
¼ tsp.	black pepper	½ tsp.
	Shaved Pecorino Romano cheese (optional)	

Skillet-Browned Broccoli with Pan-Toasted Garlic

Watch closely when toasting garlic. In a hot skillet, it can quickly go from perfectly golden to burnt.

1. Cut broccoli heads lengthwise into 1-inch slices, cutting from bottom of stems through crown to preserve broccoli shape (reserve any florets that fall away for another use). Brush both sides of broccoli slices with the 3 tablespoons oil. Sprinkle with salt and black pepper.

2. Heat an extra-large cast-iron skillet over medium heat. Place half the broccoli at a time in the hot skillet then weight with a medium-size heavy skillet. Cook 3 to 4 minutes or until browned. Turn slices over, weight them, and cook 3 to 4 minutes more or until browned. (For more tender broccoli, cook over medium-low heat for 5 to 6 minutes per side.) Remove broccoli from skillet; keep warm.*

3. If necessary, add additional oil to hot skillet; add garlic. Cook and stir over medium-low heat for 2 minutes or until lightly toasted. Sprinkle broccoli with the toasted garlic.

*TIP Keep cooked broccoli slices warm in a 300°F oven or cover with foil while cooking remaining broccoli.

FOR 16 SERVINGS In Step 1 use 6 tablespoons oil.

PER SERVING *79 cal., 5 g fat (1 g sat. fat), 0 mg chol., 174 mg sodium, 7 g carb., 2 g fiber, 3 g pro.*

START TO FINISH **30 minutes**

8 servings	ingredients	16 servings
3 large	broccoli heads with stem ends attached	6 large
3 Tbsp.	olive oil	6 Tbsp.
½ tsp.	salt	¼ tsp.
¼ tsp.	black pepper	½ tsp.
	Olive oil (optional)	
3 Tbsp.	thinly sliced garlic	6 Tbsp.

Green Beans Niçoise

Serve these dressed-up green beans—inspired by the cuisine from the French Riviera—with grilled tuna, chicken, or pork.

1. In a 4- to 5-quart Dutch oven combine potatoes, olives, the water, and shallots. Sprinkle with salt and black pepper.

2. Bring to boiling; reduce heat. Simmer, covered, 5 minutes or until potatoes are nearly tender. Stir in green beans. Simmer, covered, 3 to 5 minutes more or until potatoes are tender and beans are crisp-tender, adding tomatoes during the last 1 minute of cooking.

3. Using a slotted spoon, transfer vegetables to individual plates or a serving platter. Drizzle with oil and lemon juice; sprinkle with parsley. If desired, serve with hard-cooked eggs.

PER SERVING *133 cal., 6 g fat (1 g sat. fat), 0 mg chol., 225 mg sodium, 19 g carb., 5 g fiber, 3 g pro.*

START TO FINISH **35 minutes**

6 servings	ingredients	12 servings
12 oz.	tiny new potatoes, quartered	1½ lb.
⅓ cup	pitted Niçoise olives or firm green Greek olives	⅔ cup
⅓ cup	water	⅔ cup
¼ cup	thinly sliced shallots or chopped onion	½ cup
¼ tsp.	salt	½ tsp.
¼ tsp.	black pepper	½ tsp.
12 oz.	green beans, trimmed if desired	1½ lb.
2 cups	grape tomatoes, halved	4 cups
1 Tbsp.	olive oil	2 Tbsp.
1 Tbsp.	lemon juice	2 Tbsp.
1 Tbsp.	snipped fresh Italian parsley or basil	2 Tbsp.
	Sliced hard-cooked eggs (optional)	

Carrot Ribbon Salad

Shaving carrots into ribbons produces a great aesthetic. It's not necessary to use a mandolin or other special tool—just grab your vegetable peeler and get shaving.

1. Using a vegetable peeler, peel carrots, removing just the outer layer. Then hold carrot by the thicker end and peel carrots lengthwise into thin strips.

2. In a large bowl combine carrots, peas, and green onions. For dressing, in a small bowl combine honey, vinegar, salt, and black pepper

3. Pour dressing over vegetables; toss gently. Cover and chill for 2 to 4 hours.

PER SERVING *81 cal., 0 g fat, 0 mg chol., 151 mg sodium, 19 g carb., 2 g fiber, 2 g pro.*

PREP **20 minutes**
CHILL **2 hr.**

6 servings	ingredients	12 servings
8 oz.	large carrots	1 lb.
1 cup	frozen peas, thawed	2 cups
½ cup	thinly sliced green onions	1 cup
¼ cup	honey	½ cup
2 Tbsp.	white wine vinegar	¼ cup
¼ tsp.	salt	½ tsp.
⅛ tsp.	black pepper	¼ tsp.

Beets and Greens Salad

For best flavor, look for small firm beets with smooth skin. If you use red beets, wear kitchen gloves when peeling them to avoid staining your hands.

1. Place whole beets in a microwave-safe casserole; add vinegar, sugar, and the water. Microwave, covered, on high for 9 to 12 minutes or until beets are tender, stirring once. Remove beets, reserving liquid in casserole. Trim stems and slip off skins. Slice beets.

2. For dressing, whisk oil, salt, and pepper into the reserved cooking liquid. In a large bowl toss together beets, salad greens, and dried cranberries. Pour dressing over salad; toss gently to coat. If desired, sprinkle with pumpkin seeds and cheese.

PER SERVING *100 cal., 6 g fat (1 g sat. fat), 0 mg chol., 161 mg sodium, 12 g carb., 2 g fiber, 1 g pro.*

START TO FINISH 30 minutes

10 servings	ingredients	20 servings
6 small	golden and/or red beets, tops trimmed	12 small
½ cup	cider vinegar	1 cup
2 Tbsp.	sugar	¼ cup
2 Tbsp.	water	¼ cup
¼ cup	olive oil	½ cup
½ tsp.	salt	1 tsp.
½ tsp.	black pepper	1 tsp.
8 cups	mixed salad greens	16 cups
⅓ cup	dried cranberries	⅔ cup
	Roasted pumpkin seeds (pepitas) (optional)	
	Crumbled goat cheese (chèvre) (optional)	

Asian Wilted Greens

Make this healthful side dish a hearty main dish by tossing in sliced or shredded grilled chicken breast or chopped roasted pork tenderloin.

1. Using a mortar and pestle, crush sesame seeds, orange peel, and sea salt until well combined and orange zest begins to release oils. Set aside.

2. Trim ends of chard stems and remove from leaves. Slice stems into ¼-inch pieces. Coarsely shred leaves and keep separate.

3. In a large skillet heat canola oil over medium-high heat. Add garlic and crushed red pepper; cook and stir about 1 minute. Add ginger and chard stems; cook about 3 minutes, stirring occasionally. Add orange juice, soy sauce, sesame oil, and chard leaves; cook and stir 2 to 3 minutes or just until leaves are tender. Stir in spinach and cook until just beginning to wilt. Remove from heat. Sprinkle with sesame seed mixture.

PER SERVING *49 cal., 3 g fat (0 g sat. fat), 0 mg chol., 324 mg sodium, 4 g carb., 1 g fiber, 2 g pro.*

START TO FINISH **30 minutes**

6 servings	ingredients	12 servings
1 Tbsp.	sesame seeds, toasted (tip, page 12)	2 Tbsp.
1 Tbsp.	finely shredded orange peel	2 Tbsp.
½ tsp.	sea salt	1 tsp.
6 oz.	red or rainbow Swiss chard	12 oz.
1 Tbsp.	canola oil	2 Tbsp.
2 cloves	garlic, very thinly sliced	4 cloves
⅛ tsp.	crushed red pepper	¼ tsp.
1 tsp.	grated fresh ginger	2 tsp.
¼ cup	freshly squeezed orange juice	½ cup
2 tsp.	reduced-sodium soy sauce	4 tsp.
¼ tsp.	toasted sesame oil	½ tsp.
one 5- to 6-oz. pkg.	fresh baby spinach	two 5- to 6-oz. pkg.

Nutty Asian Cabbage with Plums

Shredded cabbage is the base for this warm roasted side. Roasting the plums brings out their inherent sweetness.

1. Preheat oven to 425°F. In a 15×10×1-inch baking pan combine cabbage, carrots, almonds, and ginger. Drizzle with vegetable oil; toss to coat. Roast 10 minutes. Stir in plums. Roast 10 to 15 minutes more or until cabbage is wilted and beginning to brown.

2. Meanwhile, for vinaigrette, combine sesame oil, sugar, rice vinegar, soy sauce, and green onions. Drizzle over salad; toss to coat.

PER SERVING *192 cal., 13 g fat (1 g sat. fat), 0 mg chol., 86 mg sodium, 17 g carb., 5 g fiber, 4 g pro.*

PREP 20 minutes
ROAST 20 minutes

4 servings	ingredients	8 servings
1 lb.	shredded cabbage	2 lb.
1 cup	thinly bias-sliced carrots	2 cups
⅓ cup	slivered almonds	⅔ cup
1 Tbsp.	peeled and finely diced fresh ginger	2 Tbsp.
2 Tbsp.	vegetable oil	¼ cup
2	red plums or peaches, pitted and cut into ¾-inch wedges	4
1½ tsp.	toasted sesame oil	3 tsp.
1 tsp.	sugar	2 tsp.
1 tsp.	rice vinegar	2 tsp.
½ tsp.	soy sauce	1 tsp.
2	green onions, cut into 1-inch pieces	4

Citrus Salad

At wintertime growing peak, three different varieties of citrus—oranges, grapefruit, and clementines star in a salad that is as refreshing as it is colorful. Serve it along with brunch, lunch, or dinner.

1. For dressing, squeeze juice from one orange and transfer to a small bowl. Whisk in olive oil, tarragon, and mustard. Peel and thinly slice remaining oranges.

2. Layer lettuce and citrus fruit in a large serving bowl. Drizzle with dressing; toss to coat. Gently toss to mix. Sprinkle with toasted coconut.

FOR 12 SERVINGS In Step 1 squeeze juice from two oranges.

PER SERVING *211 cal., 15 g fat (7 g sat. fat), 0 mg chol., 67 mg sodium, 19 g carb., 5 g fiber, 3 g pro.*

START TO FINISH **20 minutes**

6 servings	ingredients	12 servings
3	oranges	6
¼ cup	extra virgin olive oil	½ cup
1 Tbsp.	snipped fresh tarragon	2 Tbsp.
1 Tbsp.	Dijon mustard	2 Tbsp.
2 heads	Bibb lettuce, torn	4 heads
1	pink grapefruit, peeled and thinly sliced	2
2	clementines, peeled and separated into segments	4
⅓ cup	unsweetened coconut chips, toasted (tip, page 12)	⅔ cup

Orzo and Olive Salad with Spiced Citrus Vinaigrette

Fresh arugula lend peppery flavor to this spiced pasta salad. When it's unavailable, substitute watercress. Or for milder flavor, use baby spinach.

1. In a large saucepan cook orzo according to package directions. Rinse with cold water; drain well.

2. Meanwhile, in a large bowl whisk together orange juice, mint, lemon juice, honey, olive oil, coriander, ginger, salt, crushed red pepper, and turmeric. Add drained orzo, arugula, carrots, green onions, olives, and raisins. Stir until well combined.

3. Transfer salad to a serving bowl or storage container. Cover and chill at least 2 hours or up to 24 hours.

PER SERVING *206 cal., 3 g fat (0 g sat. fat), 0 mg chol., 304 mg sodium, 40 g carb., 7 g fiber, 5 g pro.*

PREP **35 minutes**
CHILL **2 hours**

8 servings	ingredients	16 servings
1½ cups	dried whole wheat or regular orzo pasta	3 cups
½ cup	orange juice	1 cup
¼ cup	snipped fresh mint	½ cup
¼ cup	lemon juice	½ cup
2 Tbsp.	honey	¼ cup
1 Tbsp.	olive oil	2 Tbsp.
1 tsp.	ground coriander	2 tsp.
1 tsp.	grated fresh ginger	2 tsp.
½ tsp.	salt	1 tsp.
¼ tsp.	crushed red pepper	½ tsp.
¼ tsp.	ground turmeric	½ tsp.
2 cups	lightly packed fresh arugula	4 cups
1 cup	packaged fresh julienned carrots	2 cups
¾ cup	thinly sliced green onions	1½ cups
½ cup	pitted green olives, halved	1 cup
½ cup	golden raisins	1 cup

Deviled Egg Macaroni Salad

The familiar flavors of traditional deviled eggs—mayo, mustard, and paprika—meet in an easy-to-make pasta salad.

1. In a small saucepan combine onion, vinegar, and sugar. Bring to simmering, stirring occasionally. Remove from heat.

2. Cook macaroni according to package directions; drain. Rinse with cold water; drain again.

3. Meanwhile, coarsely chop one egg; set aside. Halve the remaining eggs; separate yolks from whites. Coarsely chop egg whites; set aside.

4. For dressing, place yolks in a medium bowl; mash with a fork. Stir in vinegar mixture, mayonnaise, mustard, the water, salt, paprika, and pepper.

5. In a large bowl combine macaroni, the chopped egg whites, celery, and pickles. Add dressing; toss gently to coat. Top with the reserved coarsely chopped egg. If desired, sprinkle with additional paprika and/or pepper. Serve at once or cover and chill up to 6 hours. If the salad appears bit dry after chilling, stir in a little milk.

FOR 20 SERVINGS In Step 3 coarsely chop two eggs.

PER SERVING *273 cal., 15 g fat (3 g sat. fat), 228 mg chol., 422 mg sodium, 21 g carb., 1 g fiber, 11 g pro.*

START TO FINISH **30 minutes**

10 servings	ingredients	20 servings
½ cup	thinly sliced red onion	1 cup
¼ cup	cider vinegar	½ cup
1 tsp.	sugar	2 tsp.
8 oz.	dried elbow macaroni	16 oz.
12	hard-cooked eggs	24
½ cup	mayonnaise	1 cup
3 Tbsp.	country-style Dijon mustard	6 Tbsp.
1 Tbsp.	water	2 Tbsp.
½ tsp.	salt	1 tsp.
½ tsp.	smoked paprika	1 tsp.
¼ tsp.	cracked black pepper	½ tsp.
1½ cups	very thinly sliced celery	3 cups
½ cup	chopped sweet pickles	1 cup
	Smoked paprika and/or cracked black pepper (optional)	

Roasted Tomato Pasta with Mozzarella

As tomatoes roast they caramelize and their sweetness is heightened. The juices from the roasted tomatoes also add a lot of flavor to the pasta.

1. Preheat oven to 450°F. Arrange tomato halves, cut sides up, in a foil-lined 15×10×1-inch baking pan. Sprinkle with oregano, garlic, and salt; drizzle with the ¼ cup oil. Roast tomatoes, uncovered, for 20 to 25 minutes or until lightly browned and shriveled.

2. Meanwhile, in a large pot cook pasta according to package directions; drain. In a large bowl whisk together the ⅓ cup oil, the vinegar, and pepper. Add warm pasta to bowl; toss to coat. Cool to room temperature, stirring occasionally.

3. Add tomatoes and any drippings from the pan and the mozzarella to pasta. Toss to combine. Transfer pasta mixture to a serving bowl; stir in basil. Serve at room temperature within 2 hours.

FOR 24 SERVINGS In Step use 1 two 15×10×1-inch baking pans, the ½ cup oil, and rotate pans once during baking. In Step 2 use ⅔ cup oil.

PER SERVING 297 cal., 15 g fat (4 g sat. fat), 13 mg chol., 222 mg sodium, 30 g carb., 2 g fiber, 9 g pro.

PREP **20 minutes**
ROAST **20 minutes**
COOL **30 minutes**

12 servings	ingredients	24 servings
1 lb.	red, orange, and/or yellow grape or cherry tomatoes, halved	2 lb.
2 tsp.	dried oregano, crushed	4 tsp.
3 cloves	garlic, thinly sliced	6 cloves
1 tsp.	kosher salt	2 tsp.
¼ cup	olive oil	½ cup
one 16-oz. pkg.	dried whole grain rotini pasta	two 16-oz. pkg.
⅓ cup	olive oil	⅔ cup
2 Tbsp.	white wine vinegar	¼ cup
½ tsp.	cracked black pepper	1 tsp.
8 oz.	bite-size fresh mozzarella balls or cubed fresh mozzarella	16 oz.
½ cup	snipped fresh basil	1 cup

Roasted Red Pepper Soup

Serve this bright red soup alongside hot sandwiches for dipping. Paninis, tuna melts, or grilled cheese sandwiches are all tasty companions.

1. In a large saucepan heat 1 tablespoon oil over medium heat. Add onion and garlic; cook 3 to 4 minutes or until onion is tender, stirring occasionally. Stir in broth, roasted peppers, potato, oregano, and salt. Bring to boiling; reduce heat. Simmer, covered, for 15 minutes. Remove from heat.

2. Using a handheld immersion blender, blend soup until nearly smooth. (Or let soup cool slightly. Transfer soup, one-third at a time, to a food processor or blender. Cover and process or blend until smooth. Return soup to saucepan; heat through.)

3. In a small bowl combine pesto and 1 tablespoon oil. To serve, ladle soup into bowls and drizzle with pesto.

FOR 8 SERVINGS In Step 1 and Step 3 use 2 tablespoons oil.

PER SERVING *156 cal., 9 g fat (1 g sat. fat), 1 mg chol., 616 mg sodium, 18 g carb., 3 g fiber, 2 g pro.*

PREP **20 minutes**
COOK **15 minutes**

4 servings	ingredients	8 servings
1 Tbsp.	olive oil	2 Tbsp.
1 cup	chopped onion	2 cups
4 cloves	garlic, minced	8 cloves
4 cups	low-sodium vegetable broth or reduced-sodium chicken broth	8 cups
one 12-oz. jar	roasted red sweet peppers, drained and coarsely chopped	two 12-oz. jars
1 cup	peeled and chopped potato	2 cups
2 Tbsp.	snipped fresh oregano	¼ cup
¾ tsp.	salt	1½ tsp.
1 Tbsp.	basil pesto	2 Tbsp.
1 Tbsp.	olive oil	2 Tbsp.

Zucchini-Corn Soup with Crispy Bacon

Make this soup in late summer when sweet corn and zucchini are in season and at their tastiest. Large zucchini can become bitter so use medium ones for the best mellow flavor.

1. Remove husks from ears of corn. Scrub with a stiff brush to remove silks; rinse. Cut kernels from corn cobs; set aside kernels and cobs.

2. In a 4-quart Dutch oven heat oil over medium heat. Add onion, salt, and pepper; cook about 5 minutes or until onion is tender, stirring occasionally. Stir in thyme and garlic; cook and stir about 30 seconds or until garlic is fragrant. Add broth, bay leaf, and corn cobs.

3. Bring mixture to boiling; reduce heat. Simmer, uncovered, for 10 minutes. Stir in zucchini and the corn kernels. Simmer, uncovered, for 5 minutes more or just until zucchini is tender. Remove and discard corn cobs and bay leaf. Sprinkle each serving with bacon.

*TIP To make this soup even faster, use 1½ cups frozen whole kernel corn, thawed, in place of the ears of corn. Prepare as directed, except omit Step 1. With frozen corn, the soup will have a slightly thinner consistency.

PER SERVING *115 cal., 5 g fat (1 g sat. fat), 6 mg chol., 453 mg sodium, 13 g carb., 2 g fiber, 6 g pro.*

START TO FINISH **35 minutes**

6 servings	ingredients	12 servings
3	ears of corn*	6
1 Tbsp.	olive oil	2 Tbsp.
½ cup	finely chopped onion	1 cup
¾ tsp.	salt	1½ tsp.
½ tsp.	freshly ground black pepper	1 tsp.
2 tsp.	snipped fresh thyme	4 tsp.
2 cloves	garlic, minced	4 cloves
5 cups	low-sodium chicken broth	10 cups
1	bay leaf	2
2 medium	zucchini, quartered lengthwise and sliced ¼ to ½ inch thick	4 medium
4	slices bacon, crisp-cooked, drained, and crumbled	8

CHAPTER 6

Desserts

Look here for sweet ends to meal times or special occasions. From decadent to seasonal, from kid friendly to homestyle, all are impressively delicious.

163

171

173

Spice Cake with Cooked Coconut Topping

A little bit of nutmeg goes a long way, and the spice pairs well with other warm spices. For superior flavor, grate whole nutmeg rather than using ground nutmeg, which quickly loses its potency.

1. Preheat oven to 350°F. Grease and flour an 8×8-inch baking pan.

2. In a large bowl combine first six ingredients (through nutmeg). Add milk, the ¼ cup butter, egg, and vanilla. Beat with a mixer on low until combined. Beat on medium for 1 minute. Pour batter into the prepared pan.

3. Bake 25 to 30 minutes or until a toothpick inserted in center comes out clean.

4. Meanwhile, for topping, in a small saucepan combine the 3 tablespoons butter, the coconut, the ⅓ cup brown sugar, and the 1 tablespoon milk. Cook and stir over medium heat until thickened and bubbly. Stir in walnuts. Spoon over hot cake. Cool cake in pan on a wire rack.

FOR 16 SERVINGS Use a 13×9-inch baking pan. In Step 2 use ½ cup butter. In Step 4 use 6 tablespoons butter, the ⅔ cup brown sugar, and the 2 tablespoons milk.

* If desired, for 8 servings, use ¼ teaspoon ground cinnamon in place of the nutmeg. For 16 servings, use ½ teaspoon ground cinnamon in place of the nutmeg.

PER SERVING *343 cal., 16 g fat (8 g sat. fat), 52 mg chol., 288 mg sodium, 47 g carb., 1 g fiber, 5 g pro.*

PREP 30 minutes
BAKE 25 minutes
COOL 2 hours

8 servings	ingredients	16 servings
1⅓ cups	all-purpose flour	2⅔ cups
⅓ cup	granulated sugar	⅔ cup
⅓ cup	packed brown sugar	⅔ cup
1½ tsp.	baking powder	1 Tbsp.
½ tsp.	baking soda	1 tsp.
½ tsp.	grated whole nutmeg	1 tsp.
⅔ cups	milk	1⅓ cups
¼ cup	butter, softened	½ cup
1	egg, room temperature	2
1 tsp.	vanilla	2 tsp.
3 Tbsp.	butter	6 Tbsp.
½ cup	flaked coconut	1 cup
⅓ cup	packed brown sugar	⅔ cup
1 Tbsp.	milk	2 Tbsp.
⅓ cup	chopped walnuts, toasted (tip, page 12)	⅔ cup

Apple Coffee Cake

The best baking apples have just the right balance of sweet and tart, plus texture that holds up in the oven. Jonathan, Honey-Crisp, and Braeburn apples are good options for this cake.

PREP 35 minutes
BAKE 40 minutes

9 servings	ingredients	18 servings
1½ to 2 cups	chopped, peeled apples	3 to 4 cups
¼ cup	water	½ cup
1¼ cups	sugar	2½ cups
2 Tbsp.	cornstarch	¼ cup
1½ cups	all-purpose flour	3 cups
½ tsp.	baking powder	1 tsp.
¼ tsp.	baking soda	½ tsp.
¼ cup	butter	½ cup
1	egg, lightly beaten	2
½ cup	buttermilk or sour milk*	1 cup
½ tsp.	vanilla	1 tsp.
¼ cup	all-purpose flour	½ cup
2 Tbsp.	butter	¼ cup

1. For filling, in a medium saucepan combine apples and the water. Bring to boiling; reduce heat. Simmer, covered, about 5 minutes or until apples are tender. Combine ¼ cup of the sugar and the cornstarch; stir into apples. Cook and stir over medium heat until thickened and bubbly. Cook and stir 2 minutes more; remove from heat.

2. Preheat oven to 350°F. In a medium bowl combine the 1½ cups flour, ¾ cup of the sugar, baking powder, and baking soda. Cut in ¼ cup butter until mixture resembles coarse crumbs. Make a well in the center of flour mixture.

3. In a bowl combine egg, buttermilk, and vanilla. Add egg mixture all at once to flour mixture. Stir just until moistened. Spread half the batter into an ungreased 8×8-inch baking pan. Gently spread filling over batter. Drop remaining batter in small mounds onto filling.

4. In a bowl stir together the ¼ cup flour and remaining sugar. Cut in the 2 tablespoons butter until mixture resembles coarse crumbs. Sprinkle over coffee cake. Bake 40 to 45 minutes or until golden. Serve warm.

FOR 18 SERVINGS In Step 1 use ½ cup of the sugar. In Step 2 use the 3 cups flour and 1½ cups sugar. Cut in the ½ cup butter. In Step 3 use a 13×9-inch baking pan. In Step 4 use ½ cup flour and ¼ cup butter. Bake 45 to 50 minutes or until golden.

*TIP For ½ cup sour milk, place 1½ teaspoons lemon juice or vinegar in a glass measuring cup. Add milk to equal ½ cup. Let stand 5 minutes before using. For 1 cup sour milk, use 1 tablespoon lemon juice or vinegar and add enough milk to equal 1 cup.

PER SERVING *298 cal., 9 g fat (5 g sat. fat), 44 mg chol., 126 mg sodium, 52 g carb., 1 g fiber, 4 g pro.*

Earl Grey-Maple Gingerbread with Pumpkin Ice Cream

PREP 45 minutes FREEZE 4 hours
BAKE 40 minutes COOL 30 minutes

10 servings	ingredients	20 servings
½ qt. (2 cups)	vanilla ice cream, slightly softened	1 qt. (4 cups)
⅓ cup	canned pumpkin	⅔ cup
1½ tsp.	orange liqueur or orange juice	1 Tbsp.
¾ tsp.	pumpkin pie spice	1½ tsp.
1	egg, lightly beaten	2
1 cup	pure maple syrup	2 cups
1 cup	sour cream	2 cups
¼ cup	butter, melted	½ cup
2⅓ cups	all-purpose flour	4⅔ cups
1 Tbsp.	Earl Grey tea leaves, ground	2 Tbsp.
1 tsp.	ground ginger	2 tsp.
1 tsp.	baking soda	2 tsp.
½ tsp.	salt	1 tsp.

If loose Earl Grey tea is unavailable, open tea bags for the amount of tea leaves for this cake. Use a spice grinder or mortar and pestle to grind the tea leaves before adding them to the batter.

1. For Pumpkin Ice Cream, in a large bowl combine slightly softened ice cream, the pumpkin, orange liqueur, and pumpkin pie spice. Beat with a mixer on medium until combined. Spoon ice cream into a freezer container. Cover and freeze at least 4 hours before serving.

2. Preheat oven to 350°F. Grease and lightly flour an 8×8-inch baking pan.

3. In a medium bowl stir together egg, maple syrup, sour cream, and melted butter. In a large bowl stir together flour, ground tea, ginger, baking soda, and salt. Add egg mixture to flour mixture; stir until well combined. Spread batter into prepared pan.

4. Bake 40 to 45 minutes or until a toothpick comes out clean. Cool in pan on wire rack for 30 minutes. Serve warm with Pumpkin Ice Cream.

FOR 20 SERVINGS Use a 13×9-inch baking pan and bake 45 to 50 minutes or until a toothpick comes out clean.

PER SERVING *341 cal., 12 g fat (7 g sat. fat), 56 mg chol., 324 mg sodium, 52 g carb., 1 g fiber, 5 g pro.*

Chocolate Zucchini Bread

For the most tender bread, stir wet ingredients into dry ingredients just until combined. Overmixing causes quick breads to become tough and dense.

1. Preheat oven to 350°F. Grease the bottom and ½ inch up the sides of an 8×4-inch loaf pan. In a large bowl stir together flour, baking powder, cinnamon, and salt. Make a well in the center; set aside.

2. In another bowl combine egg, zucchini, sugar, oil, and vanilla. Add zucchini mixture all at once to flour mixture. Stir just until moistened (batter should be lumpy). Fold in half the chocolate pieces and, if desired, the nuts. Pour batter into the prepared loaf pans.

3. Bake 55 minutes or until a toothpick comes out clean. Cool in pan for 10 minutes. Remove loaf from pan; cool on wire rack.

4. In a small saucepan melt the remaining chocolate pieces over low heat, stirring constantly. Drizzle over bread. Wrap and store overnight before slicing.

FOR 28 SERVINGS Use two 8×4-inch loaf pans.

PER SERVING *223 cal., 11 g fat (2 g sat. fat), 16 mg chol., 130 mg sodium, 30 g carb., 1 g fiber, 2 g pro.*

PREP 25 minutes BAKE 55 minutes
COOL 10 minutes STAND overnight

14 servings	ingredients	28 servings
1½ cups	all-purpose flour	3 cups
1½ tsp.	baking powder	1 Tbsp.
¾ tsp.	ground cinnamon	1½ tsp.
½ tsp.	salt	1 tsp.
1	egg, lightly beaten	2
1¼ cups	coarsely shredded, unpeeled zucchini	2½ cups
1 cup	sugar	2 cups
½ cup	vegetable oil	1 cup
1 tsp.	vanilla	2 tsp.
⅔ cup	dark chocolate pieces	1⅓ cups
½ cup	chopped walnuts or pecans (optional)	1 cup

Bananas Suzette over Pound Cake

For this elegant but easy dessert, choose bananas that are mostly ripe yet green in some spots. Overripe banana slices become mushy when cooked.

1. Cut pound cake into four slices. In a medium skillet melt half the butter over medium heat. Add pound cake slices; cook 1 to 2 minutes or until browned, turning once. Remove from skillet.

2. Peel bananas; cut each banana diagonally into eight pieces. In the same skillet combine sugar, liqueur, orange juice, and remaining butter. Cook and stir about 1 minute or until butter is melted and sugar begins to dissolve. Add bananas; cook 2 to 4 minutes more or just until bananas are tender, stirring once. Stir in nutmeg.

3. To serve, place small scoops of ice cream on pound cake slices. Top with banana sauce.

FOR 8 SERVINGS Cut pound cake into eight slices.

PER SERVING *394 cal., 18 g fat (11 g sat. fat), 74 mg chol., 229 mg sodium, 53 g carb., 2 g fiber, 4 g pro.*

START TO FINISH **15 minutes**

4 servings	ingredients	8 servings
½	10.75-oz. loaf frozen pound cake, thawed	1
2 Tbsp.	butter	¼ cup
2	medium ripe, firm bananas	4
3 Tbsp.	sugar	6 Tbsp.
2 Tbsp.	orange liqueur or orange juice	¼ cup
2 Tbsp.	orange juice	¼ cup
⅛ tsp.	ground nutmeg	¼ tsp.
1 cup	vanilla ice cream	2 cups

Chocolate-Strawberry Shortcake Sliders

The tried-and-true flavor combination of chocolate and strawberries is presented deliciously in miniature shortcakes.

1. Preheat oven to 450°F. In a medium bowl combine sliced strawberries and half the sugar.

2. For shortcakes, in a medium mixing bowl combine flour, cocoa powder, remaining sugar, baking powder, and salt. Cut in butter until mixture resembles coarse crumbs.

3. In a small bowl combine egg and milk; add all at once to flour mixture and stir just until moistened. Drop dough into 18 portions on a lightly greased baking sheet.

4. Bake 5 to 7 minutes or until a toothpick inserted in centers comes out clean. Cool slightly on a wire rack.

5. Split warm shortcakes in half horizontally. In a chilled small mixing bowl beat whipping cream, the 2 tablespoons sugar, and vanilla on medium until soft peaks form. Using about half the whipped cream, spoon a little whipped cream on each shortcake bottom. Top with sweetened berries. Add shortcake tops. Top with remaining whipped cream. If desired, drizzle with chocolate-flavor syrup. Serve immediately.

FOR 18 SERVINGS In Step 1 use ½ cup of the sugar. In Step 3 drop dough into 36 portions. In Step 5 use ¼ cup sugar.

PER 2 SHORTCAKES *552 cal., 33 g fat (20 g sat. fat), 129 mg chol., 519 mg sodium, 61 g carb., 4 g fiber, 8 g pro.*

PREP 35 minutes
BAKE 5 minutes

9 servings	ingredients	18 servings
4 cups	sliced strawberries	8 cups
½ cup	sugar	1 cup
1⅔ cups	all-purpose flour	2⅓ cups
⅓ cup	unsweetened cocoa powder	⅔ cups
1 Tbsp.	baking powder	2 Tbsp.
¼ tsp.	salt	½ tsp.
½ cup	butter	1 cup
1	beaten egg	2
⅔ cup	milk	1⅓ cups
1 cup	whipping cream	2 cups
2 Tbsp.	sugar	¼ cup
1 tsp.	vanilla	2 tsp.
	Chocolate-flavor syrup (optional)	

Peach Kuchen

No need to wait until fresh peaches come into season to make this cake—thawed frozen peach slices taste just as wonderful.

1. Preheat oven to 350°F. Grease and flour a 9-inch round baking pan or 9×9×2-inch baking pan.

2. In a medium bowl mix flour, sugar, baking powder, salt, and nutmeg. Using a pastry blender, cut in the ¼ cup butter until mixture resembles coarse crumbs. Make a well in center of flour mixture. In a small bowl combine egg and milk. Add egg mixture all at once to flour mixture. Stir just until moistened (batter should be lumpy). Spread batter into prepared pan. Halve any large peach slices. Arrange peach slices in a single layer on batter.

3. For topping, in a small saucepan combine brown sugar, corn syrup, the 1 tablespoon butter, and the lemon juice. Bring to boiling. Quickly drizzle over peach slices.

4. Bake 40 to 45 minutes or until a toothpick inserted in the center of cake comes out clean. Cool in pan on wire rack 20 minutes. Serve warm with ice cream.

FOR 18 SERVINGS In Step 1 use a 13×9-inch baking pan. In Step 3 use the 2 tablespoons butter. Increase baking time to 45 to 50 minutes.

PER SERVING *410 cal., 15 g fat (10 g sat. fat), 73 mg chol., 224 mg sodium, 63 g carb., 2 g fiber, 6 g pro.*

PREP 25 minutes
BAKE 40 minutes
COOL 20 minutes

9 servings	ingredients	18 servings
1½ cups	all-purpose flour	3 cups
¾ cup	granulated sugar	1½ cups
1½ tsp.	baking powder	3 tsp.
¼ tsp.	salt	½ tsp.
¼ tsp.	ground nutmeg or cinnamon	½ tsp.
¼ cup	butter	½ cup
1	egg, lightly beaten	2
½ cup	milk	1 cup
2 cups	sliced fresh peaches or frozen unsweetened peach slices, thawed and well drained on paper towels	4 cups
⅓ cup	packed brown sugar	⅔ cup
1 Tbsp.	light-color corn syrup	2 Tbsp.
1 Tbsp.	butter	2 Tbsp.
1 tsp.	lemon juice	2 tsp.
	Vanilla or peach ice cream	

Ozark Blackberry Cobbler

Give this summertime cobbler an indulgent finish with a scoop of vanilla ice cream or a dollop of sweetened whipped cream.

1. Preheat oven to 375°F. For pastry, in a medium mixing bowl combine 1 cup of the flour and the salt; add shortening. Beat with a mixer on low until pieces are the size of small peas. Add the cold water; beat on low just until dough begins to form (15 to 20 seconds). Form pastry into a ball with hands; gently flatten. On a lightly floured surface roll pastry into an 8½-inch square. Cut several slits in pastry.

2. In a small bowl combine the ¾ cup sugar and remaining flour. Place blackberries and almond extract in an 8×8×2-inch baking pan. Sprinkle sugar mixture over blackberries; toss to coat. Dot butter pieces over blackberries. Place pastry on blackberries. Sprinkle the 1 tablespoon sugar over pastry.

3. Bake 45 to 50 minutes or until blackberry filling is bubbly and pastry is golden. Cool slightly on a wire rack. Serve warm.

FOR 12 SERVINGS In Step 1 use 2 cups flour and roll pastry into a 13½ × 9½-inch rectangle. In Step 2 use the 1½ cups sugar and a 13×9-inch baking pan. Increase baking time to 50 to 55 minutes.

***TIP** If desired, for 6 servings use 3 cups fresh blackberries in place of frozen blackberries. For 12 servings use 6 cups fresh blackberries in place of frozen blackberries.

PER SERVING *383 cal., 16 g fat (5 g sat. fat), 10 mg chol., 126 mg sodium, 59 g carb., 4 g fiber, 4 g pro.*

PREP **20 minutes**
BAKE **45 minutes**

6 servings	ingredients	12 servings
1¼ cups	all-purpose flour	2½ cups
¼ tsp.	salt	½ tsp.
⅓ cup	shortening	⅔ cup
3 Tbsp.	cold water	6 Tbsp.
¾ cup	sugar	1½ cups
one 16-oz. pkg.	frozen unsweetened blackberries*	two 16-oz. pkg.
⅛ tsp.	almond extract	¼ tsp.
2 Tbsp.	butter, cut into small pieces	¼ cup
1 Tbsp.	sugar	2 Tbsp.

Sherried Cherry Crisp

PREP 25 minutes
STAND 30 minutes
BAKE 50 minutes

6 servings	ingredients	12 servings
½ cup	dried tart red cherries	1 cup
⅓ cup	dry sherry or port wine	⅔ cup
4 cups	fresh* or frozen unsweetened pitted tart red cherries or sweet cherries	8 cups
1	orange	2
½ cup	granulated sugar	1 cup
1 to 2 Tbsp.	all-purpose flour**	2 to 4 Tbsp.
¾ cup	all-purpose flour	1½ cups
½ cup	regular rolled oats	1 cup
½ cup	packed brown sugar	1 cup
½ tsp.	salt	1 tsp.
½ tsp.	vanilla	1 tsp.
⅓ cup	cold butter, cut up	⅔ cup
	Vanilla ice cream (optional)	

As a substitute for dry sherry or port wine in this crisp, use apple, white grape, or cherry juice.

1. Soak dried cherries in sherry for 30 minutes. If using frozen cherries, let cherries thaw 30 to 45 minutes or until partially thawed. Meanwhile, lightly grease a 1½-quart baking dish.

2. Preheat oven to 375°F. Remove 1 teaspoon zest and squeeze 2 tablespoons juice (if using frozen cherries) or 4 tablespoons juice (if using fresh cherries) from orange. In a medium bowl combine zest and juice, the fresh or thawed cherries, granulated sugar, and flour. Stir in dried cherries with sherry. Pour into prepared baking dish.

3. For topping, in a large bowl combine the ¾ cup flour, the oats, brown sugar, and salt. Sprinkle with vanilla. Using a pastry blender, cut in butter until mixture resembles coarse crumbs. Sprinkle over cherry filling.

4. Bake 50 minutes or until filling is bubbly and topping is golden brown. Serve warm and, if desired, with vanilla ice cream.

FOR 12 SERVINGS In Step 1 use a 3-quart baking dish. In Step 2 remove 2 teaspoons zest and squeeze ½ cup juice from orange (if using fresh cherries) or ¼ cup juice (if using frozen cherries). In Step 3 use 1½ cups flour.

***TIP** For 6 servings use 1¼ to 1½ pounds fresh cherries to get 4 cups pitted cherries. For 12 servings use 2½ to 3 pounds fresh cherries to get 8 cups pitted cherries.

****TIP** If using fresh cherries, use 1 tablespoon flour and ¼ cup orange juice. If using frozen cherries, use 2 tablespoons flour and 2 tablespoons orange juice.

PER SERVING *427 cal., 11 g fat (7 g sat. fat), 27 mg chol., 295 mg sodium, 78 g carb., 4 g fiber, 4 g pro.*

Blackberry-Apricot Slump

A slump—also called a "grunt"—is a traditional New England dessert of stewed fruit topped with biscuits. This version combines lambic-style Belgian beer with fresh blackberries and dried apricots.

1. In a 3-quart saucepan combine lambic, blackberries, apricots, and ½ cup of the sugar. Bring to boiling; reduce heat. Cover and simmer for 5 minutes.

2. Meanwhile, for topping, in a bowl combine flour, the remaining sugar, the baking powder, and salt. Cut in butter until mixture resembles coarse crumbs. Add milk and sage to flour mixture, stirring just until moistened. Drop topping into six mounds on hot filling. Cover and simmer about 15 minutes or until a toothpick inserted in topping comes out clean. Serve warm and, if desired, with whipped cream.

FOR 12 SERVINGS In Step 1 use a 5- to 6-quart Dutch oven and use 1 cup sugar.

PER SERVING *277 cal., 6 g fat (4 g sat. fat), 16 mg chol., 234 mg sodium, 51 g carb., 4 g fiber, 3 g pro.*

PREP 25 minutes
COOK 20 minutes

6 servings	ingredients	12 servings
1 cup	desired-flavor lambic beer, hard cider, or fruit-flavor beer	2 cups
2 cups	fresh or frozen blackberries	4 cups
¾ cup	dried apricots, quartered	1½ cups
¾ cup	sugar	1½ cups
¾ cup	all-purpose flour	1½ cups
1 tsp.	baking powder	2 tsp.
¼ tsp.	salt	½ tsp.
3 Tbsp.	butter	6 Tbsp.
⅓ cup	milk	⅔ cup
1 Tbsp.	snipped fresh sage	2 Tbsp.
	Whipped cream (optional)	

Pecan Pan Pie

This recipe adapts classic pecan pie into easy-to-make bar cookies. The tender shortbread crust contrasts perfectly to the gooey filling.

1. Preheat oven to 350°F. Line an 8-inch square baking pan with foil; grease foil. In a large bowl stir together flour, granulated sugar, and salt. Using a pastry blender, cut in ⅓ cup butter until mixture resembles fine crumbs. Press into prepared pan. Bake 15 to 18 minutes or until light brown.

2. In a medium saucepan combine brown sugar, corn syrup, and ¼ cup butter. Bring to boiling over medium heat, stirring constantly. Remove from heat.

3. In a medium bowl lightly beat eggs. Gradually stir about ½ cup of the hot mixture into eggs. Return all of the egg mixture to saucepan. Stir in pecans and vanilla. Pour over baked crust.

4. Bake 30 to 32 minutes or until filling is set. Cool in pan on a wire rack.

FOR 20 SERVINGS In Step 1 use a 13×9-inch baking pan and cut in the ¾ cup butter. In Step 2 use ½ cup butter.

PER SERVING *363 cal., 23 g fat (9 g sat. fat), 75 mg chol., 175 mg sodium, 39 g carb., 2 g fiber, 4 g pro.*

PREP **25 minutes**
BAKE **45 minutes**

9 servings	ingredients	20 servings
1 cup	all-purpose flour	2 cups
¼ cup	granulated sugar	½ cup
dash	salt	⅛ tsp.
6 Tbsp.	butter	¾ cup
½ cup	packed brown sugar	1 cup
½ cup	light-color corn syrup	1 cup
¼ cup	butter	½ cup
2	eggs	4
1¼ cups	finely chopped pecans	2½ cups
½ tsp.	vanilla	1 tsp.

Candy-Crunch Peanut Butter Bars

Although French burnt peanuts top these dense chewy no-bake bars, other peanutty toppings work equally well. For a salty-sweet flavor combo, top them with salted peanuts. Or sprinkle honey-roasted peanuts.

1. Line an 8-inch square baking pan with foil, extending foil over edges of pan; set aside. For crust, in a food processor combine peanut butter cookies and salt. Cover and process until fine crumbs form. Add the melted butter. Cover and process by pulsing just until combined. Press mixture into prepared baking pan.

2. In a large mixing bowl beat powdered sugar, the ⅔ cup peanut butter, the softened butter, and whipping cream with a mixer on low to medium until smooth. Stir in the ¼ cup peanuts. Carefully spread over crust.

3. In a small heavy saucepan stir chocolate pieces and the ¼ cup peanut butter over low heat until melted. Spread over layers in pan. Sprinkle with additional peanuts.

4. Cover and chill about 1 hour or until set. Using edges of foil, lift uncut bars out of pan. Cut into bars.

FOR 48 SERVINGS Use a 13×9-inch baking pan. In Step 2 use the 1⅓ cups peanut butter. In Step 3 use the ½ cup peanut butter.

PER SERVING *182 cal., 12 g fat (5 g sat. fat), 11 mg chol., 127 mg sodium, 17 g carb., 1 g fiber, 4 g pro.*

PREP **30 minutes**
CHILL **1 hour**

24 servings	ingredients	48 servings
15	peanut butter sandwich cookies with peanut butter filling	30
⅛ tsp.	salt	¼ tsp.
¼ cup	butter, melted	½ cup
1 cup	powdered sugar	2 cups
⅔ cup	creamy peanut butter	1⅓ cups
¼ cup	butter, softened	½ cup
1 Tbsp.	whipping cream	2 Tbsp.
¼ cup	finely crushed French burnt peanuts or other candy-coated peanuts	½ cup
½ cup	semisweet chocolate pieces	1 cup
¼ cup	creamy peanut butter	½ cup
	Coarsely crushed peanuts with crunchy sugar coating (French burnt peanuts) or other candy-coated peanuts	

Jumbo Marshmallow Treats

Traditional marshmallow cereal treats are gussied up with smooth-as-silk marshmallow creme, then topped with chocolatey and colorful sprinkles.

PREP 25 minutes
STAND at least 8 hours

6 servings	ingredients	12 servings
3 Tbsp.	butter	⅓ cup
one 10-oz. pkg.	tiny marshmallows	two 10-oz. pkg.
one 13-oz. jar	marshmallow creme	two 13-oz. jars
1½ tsp.	vanilla	1 Tbsp.
¼ tsp.	salt	½ tsp.
7½ cups	crisp rice cereal	15 cups
½ cup	multicolor sprinkles	1 cup

1. Line an 8-inch square baking pan with foil, extending foil over edges. Lightly butter foil.

2. In a 3½- to 4½-quart Dutch oven melt butter over low heat. Add marshmallows; stir until melted. Stir in marshmallow creme, vanilla, and salt. Remove from heat. Set aside ½ cup of the marshmallow mixture. Gently stir cereal into remaining marshmallow mixture.

3. Transfer cereal mixture to prepared pan; use buttered waxed paper to press firmly. Spread reserved marshmallow mixture over cereal layer; top with sprinkles.

4. Weight uncut bars by covering the surface with a sheet of waxed paper and a sheet of foil so layers press together. Place another same-size baking pan on top of cookies; add a few cans of food for weight. Let stand at least 8 hours. Using the edges of foil, lift uncut bars out of pan. Using a buttered knife, cut into bars.

FOR 12 SERVINGS Use a 13×9-inch baking pan. In Step 2 use a 6- to 8-quart Dutch oven and set aside 1 cup of the marshmallow mixture.

PER SERVING *601 cal., 9 g fat (3 g sat. fat), 14 mg chol., 367 mg sodium, 132 g carb., 0 g fiber, 4 g pro.*

Black and White Cookies

These cookies are a New York City favorite. The dough is prepared in the same manner as cake batter, giving the cookies extra-tender sponge-like texture.

1. In a medium bowl stir together flour, baking soda, and salt.

2. In a large bowl beat butter with a mixer on medium for 30 seconds. Add granulated sugar. Beat on medium to high for 1 minute, scraping bowl as needed. Beat in eggs. Add flour mixture and buttermilk alternately, beating on low after each just until combined. Cover and chill dough for 2 hours.

3. Preheat oven to 350°F. Line cookie sheets with parchment paper. Use a ¼ cup measure to drop dough 3 inches apart onto cookie sheets (dough will be sticky). With floured fingers, flatten dough to 3-inch circles.

4. Bake 10 minutes or until edges are firm and light brown. Cool on cookie sheet 5 minutes. Transfer cookies to a wire rack to cool.

5. In a medium bowl stir together powdered sugar, 3 tablespoons milk, corn syrup, and vanilla. Transfer ½ cup of the mixture to a small bowl; stir in cocoa powder and remaining milk. Add additional milk, ½ teaspoon at a time, if necessary to make each frosting of a thick glazing consistency.

6. Spread half of each cookie with white icing. Spread remaining half with chocolate icing; let stand until set (about 1 hour).

FOR 12 SERVINGS In Step 5 use 6 tablespoons milk. Transfer 1 cup of the mixture to a bowl; stir in cocoa powder.

PER SERVING *379 cal., 10 g fat (6 g sat. fat), 51 mg chol., 351 mg sodium, 70 g carb., 1 g fiber, 4 g pro.*

PREP **45 minutes** CHILL **2 hours**
BAKE **10 minutes per batch**
STAND **1 hour**

14 servings	ingredients	28 servings
2½ cups	all-purpose flour	5 cups
1 tsp.	baking soda	2 tsp.
1 tsp.	salt	2 tsp.
⅔ cup	butter, softened	1⅓ cups
1 cup	granulated sugar	2 cups
2	eggs	4
½ cup	buttermilk	1 cup
4 cups	powdered sugar	8 cups
¼ cup	milk	½ cup
2 Tbsp.	light-color corn syrup	¼ cup
2 tsp.	clear vanilla or vanilla	4 tsp.
3 Tbsp.	unsweetened cocoa powder	6 Tbsp.
	Milk	

S'more Cookies

Enjoy the flavors of the campout favorite anytime you like—no camp fire required.

1. In a medium bowl combine oats, flour, crushed graham crackers, baking soda, baking powder, cinnamon, and salt.

2. In a large bowl beat butter with a mixer on medium to high for 30 seconds. Add brown sugar and granulated sugar. Beat on medium until combined, scraping sides of bowl occasionally. Beat in egg, milk, and vanilla until combined. Beat in as much of the flour mixture as you can with the mixer. Stir in any remaining flour mixture until combined.

3. Cover bowl with plastic wrap and chill for 1 hour but no longer than 4 hours.

4. Preheat oven to 375°F. Lightly grease cookie sheets or line with parchment paper. Drop dough from rounded tablespoons about 2 inches apart onto prepared cookie sheets.

5. Bake 8 minutes. Remove from oven. Using the back of a measuring teaspoon, make a slight impression in the center of each cookie. Place marshmallow crème in a resealable plastic bag. Seal bag and snip off a tiny corner of the bag. Pipe about 1 teaspoon marshmallow crème into the center of each cookie. Push a Kiss chocolate into center of marshmallow crème, pointed side down. Return cookies to oven. Bake 2 or 3 minutes more or until edges are light brown. Cool on cookie sheets 1 minute. Transfer to wire racks to cool.

PER SERVING *165 cal., 7 g fat (4 g sat. fat), 23 mg chol., 134 mg sodium, 24 g carb., 1 g fiber, 3 g pro.*

PREP **35 minutes**
CHILL **1 hour**
BAKE **10 minutes per batch**

21 servings	ingredients	42 servings
2 cups	regular rolled oats	4 cups
¾ cup	cups all-purpose flour	1½ cups
½ cup	finely crushed graham crackers	1 cup
½ tsp.	baking soda	1 tsp.
½ tsp.	baking powder	1 tsp.
½ tsp.	ground cinnamon	1 tsp.
¼ tsp.	salt	½ tsp.
½ cup	butter, softened	1 cup
½ cup	packed brown sugar	1 cup
¼ cup	granulated sugar	½ cup
1	eggs	2
2 Tbsp.	milk	¼ cup
1½ tsp.	vanilla	1 Tbsp.
half 7-oz. jar	marshmallow crème	one 7-oz. jar
21	Kisses milk chocolates with caramel, peanut butter, and/or almonds	42

Mini Apple Crisp Bites

For parties and potlucks, these bite-size treats are an easy-to-serve alternative to apple crisp.

1. Preheat oven to 350°F. Grease twenty-four 1¾-inch muffin cups; set aside.

2. For apple filling, in a medium saucepan combine chopped apples, apple juice, granulated sugar, and half the apple pie spice. Bring to boiling; reduce heat. Simmer, uncovered, for 5 to 8 minutes or until apples are tender. Remove from heat.

3. For streusel, in a food processor combine flour, half the oats, the brown sugar, and remaining apple pie spice. Cover and process to combine. Add butter; cover and process until mixture resembles coarse crumbs. Stir in remaining oats and pecans. Place 1 rounded tablespoon streusel in each muffin cup, pressing onto the bottoms and up sides of cups (patch as needed with additional streusel). There will be streusel left for topping.

4. Place about 2 teaspoons apple filling in each streusel-lined muffin cup. Sprinkle filling with remaining streusel. (Muffin cups will be very full.)

5. Bake 15 to 20 minutes or until golden brown. Cool 10 minutes. Loosen edges with a thin spatula. Remove from cups. Serve warm and, if desired, top with whipped cream and apple pieces.

FOR 48 SERVINGS Use two twenty-four 1¾-inch muffin cups or bake in batches.

PER SERVING *77 cal., 4 g fat (2 g sat. fat), 10 mg chol., 32 mg sodium, 9 g carb., 1 g fiber, 1 g pro.*

PREP **35 minutes**
BAKE **15 minutes**
COOL **10 minutes**

24 servings	ingredients	48 servings
2 cups	chopped, peeled apples (such as Braeburn, Jonagold, Pink Lady, or McIntosh)	4 cups
2 Tbsp.	apple juice	¼ cup
1 Tbsp.	granulated sugar	2 Tbsp.
½ tsp.	apple pie spice or ground cinnamon	1 tsp.
½ cup	all-purpose flour	1 cup
½ cup	regular rolled oats	1 cup
6 Tbsp.	packed brown sugar	¾ cup
½ cup	butter, cut up	1 cup
2 Tbsp.	finely chopped pecans, toasted (tip, page 12)	¼ cup
	Whipped cream or vanilla ice cream (optional)	
	Very thin apple slices, halved crosswise (optional)	

Affogato Trifles

An affogato is a scoop of ice cream topped with a shot of hot espresso. This recipe puts an elegant spin on the simple version by layering in crushed Italian cookies and topping each trifle with whipped cream.

4 servings	ingredients	8 servings
2 cups	coarsely crushed biscotti, amaretti, or other favorite cookie	4 cups
2 cups	vanilla ice cream, softened	4 cups
1 cup	whipped cream	2 cups
4 shots (¾ cup total)	hot brewed espresso or strong coffee	8 shots (1½ cups total)
1 tsp.	ground cinnamon	2 tsp.

1. In each dessert glass layer one-fourth of the crushed biscotti and one-fourth of the ice cream. Repeat with remaining biscotti and remaining ice cream.

2. Evenly divide half the crushed biscotti among dessert glasses. Top with half the ice cream. Repeat layers. Top with whipped cream. Serve with shots of espresso to drizzle over the ice cream and sprinkle with cinnamon.

PER SERVING *435 cal., 25 g fat (14 g sat. fat), 113 mg chol., 205 mg sodium, 46 g carb., 1 g fiber, 7 g pro.*

Index

Metric Information

PRODUCT DIFFERENCES

Most of the ingredients called for in the recipes in this book are available in most countries. However, some are known by different names. Here are some common American ingredients and their possible counterparts:

- Sugar (white) is granulated, fine granulated, or castor sugar.
- Powdered sugar is icing sugar.
- All-purpose flour is enriched bleached or unbleached white household flour. When self-rising flour is used in place of all-purpose flour in a recipe that calls for leavening, omit the leavening agent (baking soda or baking powder) and salt.
- Light-color corn syrup is golden syrup.
- Cornstarch is cornflour.
- Baking soda is bicarbonate of soda.
- Vanilla or vanilla extract is vanilla essence.
- Green, red, or yellow sweet peppers are capsicums or bell peppers.
- Golden raisins are sultanas.

VOLUME AND WEIGHT

The United States traditionally uses cup measures for liquid and solid ingredients. The chart (above right) shows the approximate imperial and metric equivalents. If you are accustomed to weighing solid ingredients, the following approximate equivalents will be helpful.

- 1 cup butter, castor sugar, or rice = 8 ounces = ½ pound = 250 grams
- 1 cup flour = 4 ounces = ¼ pound = 125 grams
- 1 cup icing sugar = 5 ounces = 150 grams
- Canadian and U.S. volume for a cup measure is 8 fluid ounces (237 ml), but the standard metric equivalent is 250 ml.
- 1 British imperial cup is 10 fluid ounces.
- In Australia, 1 tablespoon equals 20 ml, and there are 4 teaspoons in the Australian tablespoon.
- Spoon measures are used for small amounts of ingredients. Although the size of the tablespoon varies slightly in different countries, for practical purposes and for recipes in this book, a straight substitution is all that's necessary. Measurements made using cups or spoons always should be level unless stated otherwise.

COMMON WEIGHT RANGE REPLACEMENTS

Imperial / U.S.	Metric
½ ounce	15 g
1 ounce	25 g or 30 g
4 ounces (¼ pound)	115 g or 125 g
8 ounces (½ pound)	225 g or 250 g
16 ounces (1 pound)	450 g or 500 g
1¼ pounds	625 g
1½ pounds	750 g
2 pounds or 2¼ pounds	1,000 g or 1 Kg

OVEN TEMPERATURE EQUIVALENTS

Fahrenheit Setting	Celsius Setting	Gas Setting
300°F	150°C	Gas Mark 2 (very low)
325°F	160°C	Gas Mark 3 (low)
350°F	180°C	Gas Mark 4 (moderate)
375°F	190°C	Gas Mark 5 (moderate)
400°F	200°C	Gas Mark 6 (hot)
425°F	220°C	Gas Mark 7 (hot)
450°F	230°C	Gas Mark 8 (very hot)
475°F	240°C	Gas Mark 9 (very hot)
500°F	260°C	Gas Mark 10 (extremely hot)
Broil	Broil	Grill

*Electric and gas ovens may be calibrated using celsius. However, for an electric oven, increase celsius setting 10 to 20 degrees when cooking above 160°C. For convection or forced air ovens (gas or electric), lower the temperature setting 25°F/10°C when cooking at all heat levels.

BAKING PAN SIZES

Imperial / U.S.	Metric
9×1½-inch round cake pan	22- or 23×4-cm (1.5 L)
9×1½-inch pie plate	22- or 23×4-cm (1 L)
8×8×2-inch square cake pan	20×5-cm (2 L)
9×9×2-inch square cake pan	22- or 23×4.5-cm (2.5 L)
11×7×1½-inch baking pan	28×17×4-cm (2 L)
2-quart rectangular baking pan	30×19×4.5-cm (3 L)
13×9×2-inch baking pan	34×22×4.5-cm (3.5 L)
15×10×1-inch jelly roll pan	40×25×2-cm
9×5×3-inch loaf pan	23×13×8-cm (2 L)
2-quart casserole	2 L

U.S./STANDARD METRIC EQUIVALENTS

⅛ teaspoon = 0.5 ml

¼ teaspoon = 1 ml

½ teaspoon = 2 ml

1 teaspoon = 5 ml

1 tablespoon = 15 ml

2 tablespoons = 25 ml

¼ cup = 2 fluid ounces = 50 ml

⅓ cup = 3 fluid ounces = 75 ml

½ cup = 4 fluid ounces = 125 ml

⅔ cup = 5 fluid ounces = 150 ml

¾ cup = 6 fluid ounces = 175 ml

1 cup = 8 fluid ounces = 250 ml

2 cups = 1 pint = 500 ml

1 quart = 1 litre